SECRET WEAPON

Attract the best clients, charge what you're worth and fall in love with your work again.

GABRIELLE CHIPEUR

Secret Weapon by Gabrielle Chipeur
Published by 12Strong Ltd

GabrielleChipeur.com

© 2019 Gabrielle Chipeur

All rights reserved. No portion of this book may be reproduced in any form without permission from the publisher, except as permitted by Canadian copyright law.

For permissions contact:
hello@gabriellechipeur.com

Cover by Gabrielle Chipeur.

ISBN: 9781703200713

For Ashley, my stoic rock.

DOWNLOAD THE AUDIOBOOK FREE!

Just to say thanks for buying my book, I would like to give you the Audiobook version completely FREE!

TO DOWNLOAD GO TO:
https://gabriellechipeur.com/sw-audiobook

CONTENTS

Acknowledgments	i
Introduction	**1**
A Secret Weapon Focuses on Doing Business Better	**10**
Automating Our Business	13
Being Aware of Our Schedule	27
Creating Processes in Our Business	41
Getting Everything in Writing	54
Paying Attention to Our Finances	65
A Secret Weapon Does Great Work	**79**
Being Invested in the Outcome	82
Aiming for 92%	97
Assessing The Entire Situation	103
Sharing Our Knowledge	116
A Secret Weapon Gets the Best Clients	**130**
Following Up	133
Building a Referral Engine	146
Avoiding the More Client Trap	156
A Secret Weapon Grows as a Provider	**167**
Knowing Our Limits as a Provider	170
Productizing Our Services	185
The Value of Investing in Ourselves	198
Conclusion	**214**

ACKNOWLEDGMENTS

So many people contributed to, inspired and helped me in the writing of this book. We think a book is magically formed from a writer plugging away at a keyboard, but in reality, the support system and behind the scenes is far greater than just one person.

I'd first like to thank my family. My husband, Ashley and my two little boys, who put up with their partner and mother all of a sudden deciding to write a book and then diving in face first. Who when I told them I was writing a book, their first reaction was "of course you are." You supported me throughout this entire endeavor - cheering me on and trying to understand what it was I was doing. I love you so much for supporting this from day one.

To my sister Colette, who's always been my number one fan. I don't think I'd be the person I am today without you cheering me from the sidelines. Please don't ever stop calling just to chat and forcing me to look up from the keyboard.

To Megan, who was the first one to ever call me her Secret Weapon and who started this entire rabbit hole of a thought process. Without you this book wouldn't exist and would most certainly contain many more instances of the word 'that'.

To Pamela, Yolanda, Dianne, Clarissa, Michelle, Vicky, Cassidy and the other service providers who let me ask an unending list of seemingly trivial questions about their experiences - your help in shaping the stories and bringing these lessons to life was absolutely invaluable. Thank you so much for taking the time to talk to me and for having the courage to be vulnerable and share your stories.

A big thanks to Alex, you turned on a switch and supported me as

I built the lightbulb. Having you in my corner has brought me confidence, success and the changes both professionally and personally to make it happen. Thank you for supporting me, for making me laugh and for helping me see reality differently.

And lastly, thank YOU for reading this book. Just like I never set out to be an entrepreneur, I never thought I would be an author. And funnily enough, I could never be an author without the people reading the book. I sincerely hope this book gives you some tools to see success in your business - I can't wait to hear about it.

INTRODUCTION

Ever wonder why some service providers seem to get all the clients, the best projects, and live the dream? While you're trudging in the trenches, barely scraping by and spending all your time finding new clients?

Do you ever think they just have it lucky or they have some sort of magic skill you don't? Maybe they got in with the right crowd or took the right online course or got a big break that you're still waiting for.

But, what if I told you it wasn't any of those things?

What if the real reason you see those people doing so well is that they've embraced a way of doing business that supersedes luck and goes around the gatekeepers? They've worked to elevate themselves beyond the notion of a hired gun in their industry and have worked towards becoming their client's Secret Weapon.

What do you think you could accomplish if you knew what they know?

There's no magic formula or an insider secret to making big changes in your business. I've seen service providers go from just starting out to a booming revenue stream in very little time, and I've also seen service providers struggle it out year after year, barely making more money than the last. It's always fascinated me in what separated these two groups of people.

They had the same skills, they were all very likable people and there was little to differentiate one from the other at first glance. What was it that propelled these Secret Weapons to the top, while the rest were grabbing at the scraps left over?

In many books, you'd probably find a story here about how the author made it to a ridiculous amount of money in a short time and is willing to generously share with you their secrets because it would make them feel better to do so.

But that's not me.

I'm not one of the ones who had that meteoric rise to the top. I was one of the ones who scrounged for those scraps, year after year, time and time again - for far too long. I enviously watched others rise to the top, again and again, year after year, and felt as though I was somehow broken or there was something wrong with me, because I just couldn't figure out how to do the same.

I made mistake after mistake, learned lessons galore, and still for years, refused to take action on those lessons. It still kills me to this day how bloody stubborn I was for so long. I mistakenly assumed that there was just something special about everyone else, and I was doomed to play in the weeds for the rest of my life. I never achieved any of the big goals I would create every year or put up on my vision board. Disheartening? How about soul-sucking disappointment. That comes close to it.

It wasn't until I got to a point where I simply couldn't stand the mediocrity of it all that I realized two big things about myself and my business that were staring me in the face the whole time.

I was already the Secret Weapon

Despite never reaching any of my goals, and feeling as though I was falling behind in some sort of cosmic game of chess - I was actually running a pretty thriving business, despite me constantly standing in my own way.

I had clients who loved me. I worked on projects I loved, and I was able to do all this while caring for my kids from home and providing for them. I created a business (not an empire by any means) that was fed solely by referrals of genuinely happy clients who came to me again and again, year after year.

While I was sitting and pining out my window to somehow be the service provider that everyone loved and who got all the big publicity, I was blatantly ignoring the fact that I was already at the same level (or beyond) of those same people. Yet, here I was choosing to ignore it.

Some call it imposter syndrome, but at this point, it was me just being plain ridiculous. There was nothing inherently different between me and those other rockstars, and once I woke up, gave myself a slap and realized it, the first of many shifts started to happen in my business.

I was my biggest roadblock

Forget not having the right skills, not knowing the right people and not getting the big break. The biggest obstacle in my own way was myself. From my perfectionism to my inability to relinquish control, to the way I refused to do anything outside my comfort zone. This second realization was the hardest, and yet it cleared the way for so much more to happen as soon as I got off my own high horse and gave myself a shake.

Once I realized that when I took myself out of the equation, my business could grow - things started to move very fast. From creating systems to putting on my big girl business panties, the act of taking my own ego out of the mix was a key part in becoming the service provider who could actually deliver on those items from the goals list and vision board.

Once I realized these two things were staring me in the face and the direct cause of my stagnation, I knew I had to make some big changes in order to not stay in the same rut for the next 16 years. Because as service providers, we do get stuck in ruts don't we? We do the same things. We work on the same projects. We work with the same clients. And it can be easy to fall into a trap of thinking that this is as good as it can get for us.

But once you take stock of where you came from, and get a handle on where your internal stories originated, you're better equipped to make decisions based on your strengths and move towards your goals.

One of my biggest stories was that I wasn't a business owner, I was simply a service provider who did the work she was given, and that was that. When I started to flip that script and realize that not only was I the business owner, but I wasn't actually my business, things started to get real.

This is one thing that many service providers struggle with - we think that we're just here doing the work, doing our work. But we are in fact business owners whether we like it or not. When we examine how we started our own business, and how that leads us to the stories we play in our heads (in the background, on repeat, too low to actually hear), then we can start to bring changes to our situation in a very real way.

From service provider to business owner

I never wanted to be a business owner or even an entrepreneur. I grew up with a single mom who raised two children by creating a string of entrepreneurial ventures. From seamstress to caterer to bar owner and accountant, my mother did it all. And I hated it as a child.

With all the moving around between family members and babysitters, it left little me with a very skewed vision of what it means to be a business owner. And so I grew up knowing I absolutely, without a doubt, no way in the world ever wanted to be an entrepreneur when I grew up.

But fortune had other plans for me.

After I finished school, I proceeded to work my way through several jobs and positions at various companies - always moving up to a better position, nicer business, a higher salary. These seemed like the logical steps one takes in a career.

But all of that changed when I was 24 years old. Everything I assumed was flipped on its head as I was dragged, kicking and screaming into the world of business ownership.

It's the gateway drug to entrepreneurship, owning a business.

Even though I had no intention of the former, I ended up with the latter after accepting a contract with a Fortune 500 oil company in late 2007. I had no choice, there was no other way I could accept the contract without being an incorporated company.

I trudged my way down to a registry and signed the paperwork, paying the fees, grumbling the entire time and wondering if it really was worth it. But the opportunity was a once in a lifetime, so turning it down because of this small thing seemed childish, no matter what my upbringing and personal experiences were.

I was a business owner. But I didn't like it.

I worked quite happily for that oil company for two and a half years before my contract ended after I had my first child.

Honestly, I wasn't terribly upset that the contract was closed out. I said goodbye to the tall spires of the upgrader plant and certainly didn't miss the hour and fifteen-minute commute to work every day. But now I had a different problem altogether.

I had a new baby, I lived in a small town outside of a bigger city, and while I technically owned a company, I still had no desire to be an entrepreneur. What was going to be my plan? How was I going to help provide for my family? While my husband had a good job and we certainly weren't in dire straits, I nonetheless had to contribute for us to pay all our bills and satisfy that pesky need for food.

I started looking for jobs, which were some of the most heartbreaking experiences I've ever encountered. I was either severely overqualified for entry-level positions, or under-qualified for the art director or managerial roles I found. A senior or mid-level designer or developer role seemed to be pretty much non-existent, no matter how much I searched.

I applied for the three jobs I found that were local, within a reasonable drive from where I was, and got ready for the interviews. I went to three horrible interviews. Twelve years later, I'm still scarred from that experience.

At this point I knew I had a choice. I could either continue to slog through and find a job that fit my needs and send my child to a daycare, or I could strike out on my own. I mean, I already had a business, right? Even though my inclination was to find a job and get the security I craved, I knew deep down I did not want to leave my child and repeat the situation I experienced with my mother growing up.

So I started my transition from employee to entrepreneur. And while I did it begrudgingly, kicking and screaming along the way, I'm not the only one who feels that they've become an accidental entrepreneur.

Accidental Entrepreneurship

The stories are not surprising. The majority of service providers today are accidental entrepreneurs. Of all the service providers out in the world today, there is a large group of people who didn't ever plan on being in business for themselves. This is in direct opposition to the stories we hear online and in books about the prodigy entrepreneurs -

the ones who knew from a young age they were going to be a business owner, and took calculated and deliberate steps along the way to achieve that dream.

For many of us, it seems we floundered around, never really knowing what we were doing, until something ended up working and so we stuck with it. Perhaps you resonate with this last statement. I know I do. As soon as I decided to pursue my own business, taking it seriously and actively seeking new ways of bringing in income for my family, it was like opening a door to a whole new world. A world in which I didn't know the language. The signs were written in a dialogue I hadn't had any experience in, and it seemed as though everyone was on a street corner telling me I was doing it wrong.

As I talked to more and more service providers, I heard many different - and not so different - stories about how they came to be working for themselves. There were two main characteristics of their stories. Half came from traditional 9-5 jobs, with skills and talents in a particular area or industry. They eventually realized they could make more money doing those same skills if they set up shop for themselves and offered them with little to no overhead directly to their clients.

One woman I interviewed, Pam, told me how she was working at her job when the police stormed into the office and carried her boss out in handcuffs. Nonetheless, she knew she wasn't going to be employed there for much longer! The very next day, she had an inquiry from a colleague wanting to hire her to do the same work, but in a freelance capacity. From there, she never looked back and has been running her business for more than a decade.

The other half came from a situational need where they absolutely needed to make money or provide for their family. They then sought out whatever would come their way in terms of filling that need. Many of these stories were from women who had children, and decided that raising their children themselves was more important than finding a job, and so they sought any business venture that suited their particular circumstances.

I'm the perfect example of that second type of service provider. My situation and values drove my need to stay at home and provide for my children. And there are hundreds of stories just like these from around the world. People like you, who accidentally became an entrepreneur and now are making the most of it. But there's no reason that we should all be barely squeaking by. There's no sense in staying in one place, simply doing the work we do, again and again and not making meaningful progress. We need growth, we need to provide, and we need to find greater satisfaction in what we do, or else we run the risk of accidentally going broke.

We need to upgrade ourselves from accidental entrepreneurs to business owners, and by bringing in the mindset, behaviors, and actions of a Secret Weapon into the mix, we can thrive.

Taking your skills to the next level

When I think about the word 'up leveling' I immediately think of video games. You level up and gain more experience, more points, more health, more skills, or weapons. But what I've found in the real world is that up leveling has multiple definitions, depending on who's reading the word.

For a traditional employee, up leveling might mean to go up the corporate ladder, to gain better positions and eventually get into management. The people I spoke to about being an accidental entrepreneur almost always used this word to describe their decision.

Up leveling.

For them, this decision to open their own business, to go freelance, to start contracting, was almost always a way to expand and grow from where they were at the time. Once they got to a certain spot, the move to opening their own business seemed the only logical choice to them. So while they may not have set out in their lives to own a business, at some point, it was revealed to them as the only logical next step to take in their career.

For Yolanda, who was working as a sales associate for a company that sold HPV vaccines, her move to owning her own business came when her boss moved their operations to another country and asked her if she wanted to be a contractor rather than an employee. Yolanda told me she lucked out because she not only started her business with her first client and mentor in place, but she already had the skills she needed to reach out to new clients, there was no lag or growing pains for her.

The key to up leveling is to have a direction for momentum.

When we get past the stage of accidental entrepreneur and take the first steps to becoming a Secret Weapon, having a direction for that change and growth is essential.

Since first starting my business officially, and deciding to provide for my family on my own terms, I did a lot of random, misguided growth. There was no direction, and I suffered for it. It was only after identifying the four key areas of my business that I needed to focus on for my up leveling, did I see any sort of traction.

It's my hope that you can use these four categories of Secret Weapon business ownership to see a marked improvement in your own business. So you can get those projects you dream of, those clients you adore, and that publicity and praise you deserve.

There are far too many hired guns out there, and too many accidental entrepreneurs who haven't taken the steps to bring their business into legitimacy. And frankly, it's giving us all a bad rep. It's our job to do business better as service providers. It's our duty to create thriving businesses, so that the clients we want to work with don't get taken advantage of by others who can't provide the quality we can. And it's time to do this now.

Join me in becoming a Secret Weapon - I've learned all the lessons the hard way so you don't have to.

What to expect in this book

In writing this book I sat down to encompass where I thought the current business advice fell short when talking to people like us - people who were not only running the business, but also doing the work. There is tons of business advice out there. Advice for marketing, advice for operations, advice for managing the people in your business and advice for how to scale. But I found I had to consistently read between the lines or adjust that business advice for my own use.

In adjusting this advice for how I worked and how my business ran, I realized that they left out two key facets of a service providers business - how we grow as a service provider and how we're able to do the best work without compromising our values for the elusive idea of scaling or growth.

These were the missing pieces that once I figured them out, it left me with a clear sense of how I could grow using the advice I had received from other business mentors.

In this book you'll find there are two categories that are pretty standard - attracting clients (aka marketing) and doing business well (aka operations). The other two categories are completely my own and I feel that you'll benefit greatly by bringing this into your business repertoire.

Each category is broken into several key lessons I've learned from running my business and at the end of each chapter you'll find a TL:DR section that sums up the lessons of each chapter so you can easily reference them in the future.

Throughout the book I mention a few resources, tools or platforms that I use or have used in my business and at the end I've put these into their own resource list so you can reference them easily in the future or if you want to come back to them at a later date.

So with that being said, let's dive in shall we?

A SECRET WEAPON FOCUSES ON DOING BUSINESS BETTER

In the midst of our to-do lists and projects and things we need to do right away, there are the little things we know we should be doing. These are the tasks Stephen Covey calls the 'Important But Not Urgent' - the tasks we know will move the needle forward in our business but aren't screaming for attention like our inbox, our messenger list, and our DMs on various social media platforms.

These are the tasks which can go by day after day, week after week, and not get done but no real harm will come to you or your business. Well, that's not entirely true, no real harm will come to your business, but no real good will come of ignoring them, or putting them off until later.

These tasks and projects are the ones when complete, will make a whole hell of a lot of difference in our business in the day to day. But we can easily convince ourselves we're doing just fine without them. One of the key differences between a hired gun and a Secret Weapon, is that these Important But Not Urgent tasks will be prioritized because they see the value in making their business run smoother.

Every small thing the Secret Weapon can optimize in their business, they do. They make space for it in their weekly task list and keep them prioritized on a consistent basis. They know that the time spent *on* their business rather than *in* it will multiply in value from the moment they finish. They see the rewards from these tasks time and time again, gaining momentum to do more to optimize and run their business better.

Better. That's a subjective term, isn't it? Right now, better might mean just making sure you have a way to consistently follow up with your clients on a week by week basis. Better might mean taking a small step to getting your files in order so you can easily find what you're looking for. Better might mean creating a specific set of templates you use consistently, so you don't have to recreate them every time you get a new client

Better denotes small steps. Not big ones.

Better is not to be confused with productivity. Being productive is the act of being able to do more with the time you have. Better is taking away. Better is removing that which doesn't need to be done manually or from scratch every time. Better is less, while productivity is more.

In our search to make our business better, we often confuse the two, so I thought it important to highlight the difference here. By no means is productivity the enemy, but we should search for ways to be more productive as well. But productivity extends to our own personal work and the tasks we manually do ourselves. Better deals with the tasks and processes by which things get done outside of our direct actions.

How does a Secret Weapon make their business better? In this section of the book, we're going to dive into several strategies which have made a big difference in both my own business and in the businesses of many others.

We all need to start from somewhere.

When I was pregnant with my second child, I went on a client and project bender. Not only did I have that nesting urge, but I also had the provider urge - I needed to have a nest egg to go along with my nest. A big part of the services I did for others at the time was to help them automate and streamline so they could remove themselves from the day to day tasks of running their business. Things like admin work, client management, bookings, and payment systems. As I worked on all these projects, (frantically, methodically and with an urge to get them done so I could maybe relax a little bit once I had this tiny human), I realized everything I was working on for my clients was exactly what I needed for my own business.

The classic case of the cobbler's children, who grew up with no shoes.

Once I realized this, I hit the brakes hard and made some space in my schedule to start implementing some of the strategies and techniques I'm going to cover in the next few chapters.

The difference was astonishing.

I saved time, I saved effort, and in the end, I made more money because I wasn't wasting my precious time doing small things that ate up the majority of my work day. When you have two small children, your time is the most precious thing you could possibly have. But when you're a service provider and your time is the most literal definition of money, your time is infinitely valuable as well. Why spend that precious time on things that aren't billable?

This is what is at the heart of better for a service-based business. When you're directly charging for your time, making the most of that time is the best use of your resources and efforts. The pursuit of better over productivity makes the most amount of sense in the transition from hired gun to Secret Weapon.

AUTOMATING OUR BUSINESS

It was December 30th and I was a month late with my year-end books. I had exactly three days to get it all to my accountant, or they wouldn't be able to complete them on time, and I'd be hit with a fine I absolutely couldn't afford.

I was scrambling to get the expense receipts, banking statements, income reports, and the other items they needed the first day back after the winter holidays.

In the last four months, I had ignored the admin tasks in my business because I was slammed with client work I mistakenly thought was more important. So there I was, at the end of December when I should have been celebrating with a giant cup of heavily seasoned eggnog, but I was working furiously on the admin tasks I had put off, and the last-minute client project I mistakenly assumed I would have time for.

I was stressed, to say the least.

While usually my Decembers are pretty slow and allow me some time off for fun and relaxation, this year it was anything but. I was determined to do it all though - I needed to get this tax stuff off to the accountants, and I absolutely had to deliver on the client project.

In the end, I had to focus on the financial stuff first. I knew no matter how important that client project was, if I didn't get this admin work done, I wasn't going to be in business for much longer.

It ended up with me missing my January 1st deadline for that client's website. We ended up launching on January 3rd instead, and I definitely took a lot of heat for it. It's not my proudest moment, and it was then that I had a pretty vivid realization about my situation.

I was caught in the stereotypical service provider trap.

We do everything in our businesses - from admin, to financial, to operations, to the actual client work itself. More often than not, the work we really want to do - the creative, fun, and interesting work, gets pushed to the back burner at times when the running of our business is most important.

Balancing the act of working *in* our business (the client and project work that we love) and working *on* our business (the admin work) is a tricky balancing act for the best of people, and because we generally don't have a lot of help, we spend far too much time each week doing tasks which are anything but the work we want to do.

I don't know about you, but when I'm doing too much admin work - I tend to balk. I'll put it off and put it off, always searching for more 'fun' things to do rather than spend time doing my paperwork. I'll hide in the client work and ignore my business until it gets too big, and I can't ignore it anymore.

If you're anything like I am, the whole situation feels a bit hopeless. Both things are needed to run a service-based business - you need to do the client work, and you also need to do the admin work - there is no one or the other. But that's not why we do what we do right? We want to be doing the fun and creative work we're called to do.

How, then, do we strike a balance? How do we ensure we're free to do the work we want to, while also making sure the admin tasks that support our business get done in a timely manner?

The secret here is to use the advances of technology to help us automate the less fun parts of our business so we can focus more of our energy on the work we love to do.

But Automation Won't Work For Me

A lot of service providers I've talked to are extremely hesitant to automate parts of their business. They feel as though as a service provider since you're the one doing the work, there's no way to automate that.

And you're right.

There is no way we can automate our big beautiful brains, so that the work we do is done for us. We can't automate a designer's sense of style or a web developer's way of writing clean code. We can't automate the words being written by a professional copywriter, and it would be foolish to try to automate the tasks done by a community manager for their customers.

As service providers, we pride ourselves on being able to do everything ourselves. Many of us don't want to grow big huge businesses, but rather want to focus on what we do and doing it to the best of our ability, while working with wonderful clients.

But the fact of the matter is, when you're a solo person running a business, there are plenty of tasks that will fall into your lap that you don't enjoy, that you know you shouldn't be doing, and that you kind of dread doing on a week by week basis.

Perhaps you've entertained the idea of getting help for these tasks, but you really don't even know where to start - how do you train someone or afford them - to help you do the things you feel you barely have time to do yourself? I know I felt the same way when I first handed off my bookkeeping and accounting services to another professional. I didn't even really understand what was happening in my books, so handing those over to someone else felt scary and intimidating - how would they know what categories my expenses go in? Would they understand the intricacies of an online business? Were they trustworthy? The indecision and constant questioning can leave us feeling paralyzed and frozen instead of liberated.

And then you have the issue of the personal touch.

As service providers, we pride ourselves on the fact our clients can reach us. Not a bot, not a canned response and not someone else, when they reach out. We worry about losing the connection we have to our clients and have them get the impression they're not an important part of our business.

When we do decide to look into automation or getting some of these admin tasks off our plate, we then fear not knowing what's going on in our business at any given moment. When everything flows through us, we know where we stand and what's going on at all times. If we automate this, are we then going to be floating aimlessly around not knowing what's happening with our clients or projects because some bot is responding for us without any of our charming personality?

All of these are perfectly reasonable fears, and they point to the experiences we've had working online with businesses who did automation wrong. Businesses who went too far to the dark side of automation, instead of following a clear sense of guidelines. Businesses who didn't know how to use automations for what they were intended to do - take the work off our plate - and not replace us entirely.

Automation is Not The Enemy - Lack of Customization is

Automation can get a bad rap because so many businesses are using it incorrectly. This is especially prevalent amongst service providers. Because we tend to swing far too wide in our choices, we believe we have to either do everything ourselves or automate everything.

But that's not the case.

We need to arrive at a balance between the two, which allows us to do the best work we can, while saving us time in the areas we don't enjoy or that software can do better.

The key is not to try to automate your client work, but rather focus your automation efforts entirely on the behind the scenes of running your business. The real benefit of automation is to see where you're spending the time that could otherwise be done in a more efficient manner and automating that. Automation is best used for the tasks you don't want to do -the ones dragging you down and eating up the majority of your time.

These are things like email follow ups, invoicing, and project management, researching new ideas or tools for your business or for your clients, and even things like social media. The main focus here is you need to be doing the things that matter the most to your business. These include the work for your clients and the marketing and sales for your own business.

When I first entered into the world of automation, I heard an amazing phrase by a fellow, Sean McCabe, that has stuck with me over the years. He said you need to be using your brain as a processor and not as storage.

David Allen has a whole system devoted to being more productive and a way of organizing your daily tasks, so the important stuff gets done first. You might have tried his methods or read his books on the subject.

The most important thing I feel is glossed over in his entire system, is directly related to Sean McCabe's idea of using our brains for processing and not storage. The one tip that made the most difference in my life was to write down the things that come to my head, instead of trying to remember them later. This one idea has made a huge difference in the way I approach my day to day, and you'll often find me with a small reporter-style notebook sticking out of my back pocket. I use this to capture random ideas so I can recall them later, and I don't spend hours feeling like I forgot something (because chances are, I probably have).

Just like keeping a small notebook or writing things down, automation is there to help us take action on the things we don't need to remember on a day to day basis but are important for our business to function.

We don't have to take up brain space to remember to send an invoice. We can automate it.

We don't have to remember to send a series of follow up emails to the prospect who's still on the fence about working with us - we can automate it.

We don't have to remember when's the best time to publish our posts on Facebook or Instagram, because we can automate it.

And we certainly don't have to remember to gather up all our monthly expenses and send them to our accountant, because we can automate that too.

Don't get caught in the trap that your business is somehow unique or special and that automation won't work for you. It can and it will. One of the most common excuses I hear from service providers is that somehow their business is the exception to the rule, and almost every one of them can benefit from some sort of automation. Keep an open mind and really think about how you can use this in your business to streamline workflows and put your brain to its best use rather than a glorified storage drive.

Getting Started With Automation

The typical behavior service providers enact once we get to the point of implementing automation in our business is to do a few google searches, get overwhelmed by the possibilities, go into shut down mode and put it on the back burner for when we 'have more time.'

It's a tragedy.

Because most service providers go about it the wrong way, focusing on the steps needed to get there first rather than approaching the process in a logical manner that focuses on the end result, then works backward.

Automation takes a certain mindset for it to work effectively - one that isn't afraid of things taking a bit of time and is focused on the overall goals of a business rather than taking a narrow point of view of each small step of an automation.

The very first step when we're getting started bringing automation into our business is to focus not on what we can automate, but rather what we cannot. We have to create very solid boundaries and no-go zones around what we absolutely don't want to automate first. These are the things that absolutely need our attention, that require more finesse or need more complex problem solving to address.

Most of these tasks are the work we do for our clients. Tasks like the creation of content, the creation of our message, and the direct interaction with the people involved in our business.

For example, while we absolutely could automate the posting of our social media posts, we certainly wouldn't automate responding to people's questions or comments on our posts.

While we could certainly automate the initial delivery of invoices, contracts, and project scope documents, we most certainly would not automate responding to individual questions or responses from our clients regarding those items.

And while we definitely can automate the creation of reports and sending of factual data to our clients, the interpretation and conclusions from those reports would definitely not be something we can automate.

Are you starting to see what I mean by what we can and cannot automate in our business? Starting with what we absolutely cannot automate helps us get a better idea for the big picture and gets us clear on the automations we can create to alleviate some of the load.

Once we know what tasks and aspects of our work we can't automate, we can start creating a list of things we do each and every week that could be best automated to save us time and energy. When making this list, we can examine what tasks are ones only we can do, and which ones are something which another person could do. These second group of tasks are ones that are good candidates for automation, and lets us dip our toes without going overboard and ending up with gaps in our client experience.

Starting with one task at a time will keep the overwhelm at bay, so we don't feel as though we have to automate all the things right now. Start slowly, pick the first one, go through the process of automating it, and then move on to the next one.

Setting up Automations For Common Tasks

When I first spoke to Wendy about her web design business, she was feeling as though she was drowning in weekly admin tasks for her clients and didn't even know where to start to ease some of the load from her plate. She had about 12 consistent clients that were all on monthly maintenance retainers, and she was spending a large chunk of time each week doing the maintenance tasks, sending reports, and making sure their small requests were dealt with promptly.

She was happy about the monthly income she earned from these clients, but besides from raising her rates on the people who already had contracts in place, she didn't know what else she could do to make this more profitable for her. Every week for each client, she updated plugins and themes, sent search and analytics reports, and prided herself on knowing exactly what was going on with every site she maintained at all times.

Wendy had looked into outsourcing the tasks, but the return on it would be minimal and not worth her investment. So she just kept telling herself that it was 'just a bit of work,' Unfortunately, when we sat down and went over her hours for doing these tasks that 'bit of work' ended up being about four hours each and every week!

Wendy didn't want to raise their rates to make the amount of work more profitable for her, and I totally understand where she was coming from - so we took a different approach and examined how she could automate some of these tasks to get her back some of those four hours each week.

We first looked at the things she couldn't automate, and Wendy decided the actual updates to the sites, the plugin and theme changes, needed to be done by her so she could make sure no issues arose from them. But when we dug a bit further, we realized there was no reason she should be manually creating the weekly reports she sent to clients. Using a combination of tools, we created a reporting system where the report data was automatically pulled in from various sources into a Google Sheet, and a PDF of that Google Sheet was sent to each client on a weekly basis.

She ended up saving about two hours each week from one automation alone. Now, all it takes for her to set up a new client is to enter some preliminary data into a spreadsheet, and it automatically updates the info for her each week.

This is just one simple example of how we can use an automation to save us time on the admin side of things in our service-based business. When we step back from our tasks and objectively look at which ones could be done just as well by automation, the possibilities really are endless!

Maintaining Your Automations

Once we have your automations set up, we're free and clear, right?

Nope.

One of the most significant issues I see with automations is they're never revised, never tweaked and never adjusted for changes as a service provider grows. We need to make sure they adjust to the way we work with our clients and run our business, no matter how that looks throughout the years.

I can honestly say that if I ran my business based on the automations I had created a few years ago, I would be missing out on opportunities and still be running a bunch of stuff by hand. As the business grows, as we start to do different work, and as we discover new and interesting ways to run our projects, our automations will grow and evolve.

Beware becoming complacent with your automations because they have the potential to do damage to your reputation and leave your clients wondering if you really do have this stuff figured out.

For example, I'm a member of a Facebook group for a prominent expert in the field of Virtual Assistants. She's a great expert on the subject, and has some fantastic training, and insights into the field, plus she's got a great personality that people love. But the other day her very large audience received over 12 emails each telling them they had signed up for a specific product, then sending cancellation emails, then sending more confirmation emails and then sending more cancellations. I really felt for her because in my mind an error of that scale could absolutely have been avoided if she had been consistently managing her automations a bit better.

Though an apology email came at one point, saying that the tech gremlins had risen in her back-end systems, the damage to her reputation is very palpable. While most people are pretty forgiving, the memory of the mistake and the issues that arose from it, will certainly remain in everyone's mind, and she's lost a bit of trust from her audience.

This is even more palpable when we're doing client work. While this lady had a large audience, and was primarily doing 1 to many trainings, and online courses, if we had this happen to a client and accidentally sent them 12 emails over the course of a few hours, the damage to our reputation and perceived expertise would be done and we couldn't possibly get that back.

What can we do to make sure our automations never run amok on us? The process is rather simple, and by running through these set of actions every few months, we can save a bunch of headaches in the future.

The first part of the process is simply testing them thoroughly as a client every so often. Sign up for your discovery calls, book a session, or fill in your project planning form - what sort of emails do you get? Is the messaging correct? Does the timing of the emails make sense?

When you go through the process of a sample project, going through each phase, are the correct labels being applied? Are tasks being handled the way you want them to? Does the setup of the backend processes for each project make sense, or have you been manually tweaking them for each one just because it's a known flaw in your automation?

By taking ourselves out of the provider shoes and putting them into the client's shoes, we're able to see exactly what sort of experience they're having when they interact with us and our business. We're able to make any changes that need to be made to ensure everything is running smoothly, going forward.

Give Yourself Permission to Tweak - But Only at Certain Times

If there's one thing I would want to warn you about when setting up and enacting automations in your business it's this - don't be afraid to tweak your automations, but make sure you put limits around it.

It can be super easy to go hog wild and tweak our automations to death until we feel as though they're perfect. While a noble endeavor, it's nonetheless wasting time to attain something that is nearly impossible. Yes, we need to tweak and make adjustments as we go, but it's important to put boundaries around that need to tweak and make changes.

Set aside a specific time, once a month or once a quarter, to go through and make sure everything is working properly and that the automations are set up in a way that still makes sense. But don't constantly tweak at length. Avoid the temptation to make small changes until it's perfect - because in reality, it most certainly never will be. There will be things needing to be changed from time to time, and we can be absolutely okay with that.

Keeping Automations Running Smoothly

In a perfect world, once we set up an automation in our business that would be that and we could rest assured they'll run perfectly from now until infinity. But we all know that's an unrealistic expectation, and more often than not, things break and need to be monitored to make sure they're working correctly.

I remember in one of my projects, a client needed their online course connected to their e-commerce store and their email marketing platform. At first, the project seemed simple enough, but the further we dived into exactly what was needed to connect the three platforms,

I realized we'd need to create some heavy-duty automations to make the customer experience as smooth as possible.

I started the project and completed the various automations, feeling pretty darn proud of my advanced integration between her systems. I had identified several areas in which we could make it better and how we could work with the aging email marketing platform she was using.

My pride was short-lived; however, when later that month, she called me in a tizzy because she had a large group of customers who weren't receiving their email signup notification after purchasing their courses. They were rightly upset that they couldn't access the course they purchased.

After having a bit of a panic moment, I went into the automations to discover what could be the issues. I found some pretty significant errors and while they weren't of my creating (they were due to an unforeseen bug in the email marketing platform) they nonetheless threw a big 'ol wrench in the works.

But the big issue here wasn't that I had unknowingly discovered a pretty big bug in this platform, but rather I hadn't put into place any stopgaps to alert myself, or my client, when things went wrong. So here we were, blissfully unaware that a big percentage of her customers weren't getting these notifications, and we didn't find out until some of them complained. Realizing just how extensive the issue was made me feel pretty darn sheepish.

We can avoid this same mistake by creating stop-gap points or alert systems that will let us know right away when something doesn't go as planned.

The best way we can do this is to enable some sort of reporting for successful or erroneous completions of our automations. Most of the automation tools out there have a reporting feature where they will email if something goes wrong - I highly recommend you enable it.

How can you put some stopgaps into your automations? How can you make sure you're not in the dark about what's going on in your automations? Ensuring you have the answers to these questions will allow you to correct any issues right away, rather than when you get a complaint, or allow a client to fall through the cracks.

One Step at a Time

You know automations are important, you're clear on what you should and shouldn't be automating in your business, and you have an idea of how you're going to keep track of them, so you are alerted of any errors that arise.

You're ready to automate.

Now what?

I talked above about making a list of the tasks you could automate; now it's time to take that list and slowly turn them into useful and powerful automations for your business.

One at a time.

But why can't I just dive in and do them all at once? You may ask - and it's a valid question, because when someone gets the bug for automation, it's hard to hold back and not try to automate everything you can, right now.

When we create automations, it's incredibly important we do it one by one so that they can stack together nicely, like blocks in a Jenga tower. Since many of our automations will rely on others or on outside circumstances to trigger them, it makes the most sense to create them in a manner that builds that Jenga tower, so it's structurally sound.

There's also the very big problem of overwhelm when we start a big project like this. As we go through the process of creating our automations, we're going to find things that don't work, which need better planning, or a limitation with the software we're using. Wouldn't it be better to discover those in small pieces rather than all at once?

When I first started to bring automation into my business, when I had two little boys to take care of, I did just that - I tackled a massive pile of them at once. Little did I know there was one feature in my invoicing program I assumed was there but wasn't. I had to start from scratch, using a different platform that could accomplish what I wanted. It wasn't hard, but it was frustrating and time-consuming. Plus, since I had eight automations riding on that one feature, I had to go back to the drawing board with all of them and erase the progress I had made so far.

When we do them one by one, we give ourselves time to test, time to tweak as needed, and time to do this in and amongst our other client work and projects.

Automation can be sexy, not scary.

There are so many service providers who fear the word automation, because it means that they're losing the individual touch they feel makes them unique. But I don't really see it that way. We're simply cloning ourselves and recreating the way we do things. We're not handing the reins over to a robot who might muck things up for us.

The best automations are planned and executed, so they don't look and feel like automations to the end receiver at all. They continue to sound like us and feel like us, despite being sent by tools that take care of the nitty-gritty details.

Starting today, take steps towards bringing some automation into your business so that you can give yourself space to focus on other tasks requiring your unique skills and talents. I'm sure you'll start to see a big difference in the way your business can operate without your direct intervention on every little thing.

TL:DR

- Automation done right can be a game-changer for our business, because it lets us focus on what we do best - the creative work.
- Most service providers think that automation will take away the personal touch from their business, but as long as you keep this top of mind, you'll be fine.
- You need to use your brain as a processor, not a storage device.
- When creating automations, start with the tasks you can't automate and then work from there.
- Test your automations frequently, so that you know they're running correctly.
- Know that your automations will need tweaking and adjustments over time, but make sure to set limits around how much you tinker with them.
- Create your automations one at a time, so you can ensure that they're working correctly, and you don't get overwhelmed by doing it all at once.

BEING AWARE OF OUR SCHEDULE

If there's one thing I've noticed about the Secret Weapons I envied before I figured all this out - it was that they appeared to have the perfect balance of being booked out, and having space to balance the other areas of their lives. Some may call it work/life balance, and others call it time management, but I've realized they're both not entirely accurate to describe the situation when it comes to a service provider.

It's true, many Secret Weapons are totally booked out, in that they don't have room for any more clients or projects. It's also true Secret Weapons are very good at time management, knowing how much they can take in a day and how to schedule things, so they're not overworked or stressed out.

But I feel the underlying missing concept is the finesse Secret Weapons use to manage their schedule, and the keen awareness they have around their time. Being able to know what's on their plate, and how full that plate is at a moments' notice, is a skill worth cultivating.

When a service provider is fully aware of their project load and schedule, it gives them a sense of freedom and resolve in saying yes or no to incoming projects without having that momentary panic of, "Do I have enough to pay the bills?"

When we know our schedule, we can easily plan our projects, our personal life, downtime, and the activities to grow our business. Having this comprehensive view of our time ensures we're better able to control the expectations we have of our ourselves and others have of us.

Learning this lesson took me a long, long time - and I'll admit I still struggle with it. I'll say yes to projects I really should put off for a few weeks, and I will find myself in dead zones where I didn't properly plan for new projects coming in to keep me busy.

Up until about 2017, I would run into a scheduling problem in early January every single year. My clients and I would take a bit of a breather over the holidays, taking much needed time off and resting. Projects would be put on hold until after the holidays when new budgets and time opened up for everyone.

While December was consistently nice and relaxing, I always assumed it would pick up on the first day of January, and I'd be back in business. But it never worked out that way.

Every single year, I would be sitting there for the first few weeks of January, starting to panic because no new projects were coming in and I felt I couldn't possibly hit my sales targets or you know, pay my internet bill.

And every single year at the end of January, I would get slammed with too many projects to carry, and the next three weeks to a month were absolute hell while I struggled to fulfill them.

The culprit? Me.

Every single year I would panic in that first week of January after looking at my very empty schedule and send out all my feelers for new projects. This, of course, would lead to all my feelers coming back with projects, all at the same time. This slam of projects were all ones I felt I had to say yes to because a) I asked for them and b) there was nothing else going on in my schedule up until then.

I repeated this cycle year after year. The downtime in December, the dead zone-inducing panic in early January, and the slammed out, work until I bled sprint in February.

I usually was a wreck by the end of February every year and was pretty burnt out by the time March hit. Every single year.

Looking back at this, I have to shake my head and laugh at how predictable it was, but it's only in looking back we can see the dots of how our behaviors and actions led to the results we received.

My unawareness of my schedule, and knowing to account for these slower times rather than panicking when I realized I was in one, led me to near-collapse once a year, every year, for eight years straight. You'd think I would have learned my lesson sooner, but no, it took *eight entire years* for this one to sink in.

When I realized this was due to the nature of my industry, and my own clients (rather than some sort of January-induced failure on my part), it hit me that I had to learn to create precautions and plans, so I wouldn't fall into the yearly panic and overwhelm cycle.

Being aware of their schedule and planning accordingly is one of the key features that sets apart a Secret Weapon from other services providers. They're aware of what's coming up, what their workload looks like from week to week, month to month and they use this information to properly plan their time, so they don't get caught in dead zones or panic times.

Feast and Famine and Saying Yes

The term 'feast and famine' is probably one you've heard countless times before, more often in the negative connotation, and as something to be feared and avoided at all costs.

It's something we all strive to avoid, and it's something we shake our fists at when we're in the famine stage while groaning about busy we are when caught in the feast stage. There really is no winning when you're caught in this cycle, and most service providers feel helpless when it comes to figuring out how to break it.

The biggest culprit to the feast and famine cycle is the average service provider's inability to say no. We say yes because we want the project. We say yes because we need the revenue. We say yes because we like the client and their project excites us.

Saying yes gives us a rush, and the subsequent signing of paperwork and paying of invoices keeps us on a business high until we settle in and start to do the work. But the rush goes away pretty fast when we realize we don't actually have the time to complete that project in the timeline we promised, while having a normal sleep schedule.

But we keep saying yes.

We keep our focus on the acquisition of projects and clients, and not on the fulfillment of those projects. Since we're heavily reliant on the number of hours in a day, the amount of focus we have, and the limited energy stores we have at our disposal - we're at a disadvantage in comparison to a product-based business where these resources are more abundant.

We literally cannot get any more time. And while it's true that you and Beyoncé have the same number of hours in a day, Beyoncé is not the one creating a website for her clients, or saying yes to far too many of them to fit into an average work week.

The Appeal of Being Fully Booked Out

I have a problem with the term "fully booked out."

It's become prevalent in the online space for service providers, and while the concept is appealing on the surface, something lies underneath far more insidious than you or I could comprehend at first glance.

When we first think of the term full booked out, we may think of having no more room for more clients, and that's appealing certainly. Or we may think of having a full load of work and the money or revenue to reflect that situation. And again, nothing wrong with that.

But what we don't realize is when we're fully booked out - we have no room to breathe.

There is no space in our schedule for ourselves or our business; there is no space for us to take time off. There is no extra wiggle room for when we're just not feeling it and want to play hooky.

This puts a lot of strain on a person. It causes tremendous amounts of pressure that's not healthy in the long run for service providers and leads to burn out or worse.

This idea that if you're not fully booked out, you're somehow a failure has become so prevalent as to be obnoxious. And it's dangerous. It leads to service providers compromising on their ideals, boundaries, and healthy habits in order to achieve something which, in reality, most of them probably don't want or need in the first place.

I've been fully booked out, and I'm sure you can think back to a time when you were too. How did you feel during that time period?

If you're anything like me, you probably can't remember much from that time except a big 'ol bundle of stress and frantic busy work. Every single time I've gotten to the point where I could say I was fully booked out, was a time when I was incredibly unhappy and stressed to the nines. It was not the ideal working situation for me, and I'd hazard to guess that it's not what you want to become the norm in your business either.

What's Wrong With Being Fully Booked Out?

Let's examine the idea of being fully booked out further, and why when we're fully booked out we're not in fact, in control of our schedule. Being in control and aware of our schedule is a quality of a Secret Weapon, once we examine it, we can see why the concept of being fully booked out goes against what a Secret Weapon should be aiming for.

Everything in nature requires space to be healthy - and you, my fellow service providers, are no different. When we have space in our schedules, we're able to be flexible in ways that aren't possible with a full client load breathing down our backs, packed full of projects that need to get done right meow.

When's the last time you scheduled yourself so full, that you literally didn't have enough time to eat or sleep properly? I can think back to those days in late January and February each and every year, where taking care of myself took a back burner to the work I needed to get done. And I don't like the person I was or the quality of work I did.

When we're so full of work, it doesn't let us do our best work. And it's the quality of our work that stands out above all else. If we're working on back to back projects, with no time to brainstorm, reflect and be curious in-between, then we're not doing our best work. The space that goes in between and around projects are what makes each project better. Because we have the time to be inspired by other avenues, time to research and learn new techniques, time to be creative and explore, we have the time to make each subsequent project better than the last. When we're rushing from one job to the next, we don't have the space and time to make sure we're doing our best work.

Not having space in our schedule also raises our stress levels to the point of being unhealthy. I don't have to start lecturing you about the dangers of stress in our lives - we all know the physiological effects of stress all too well. Racing hearts, racing minds, inability to sleep properly, anxiety, and depression are just a few of the side effects of stress, and if you're a service provider, you know them all too well.

Being fully booked out brings untold levels of stress in our lives - the complete opposite of what many of the people promoting it are promising us.

This not only isn't fair to us - it's unfair to our clients. If you were to hire someone for your job, and knew you had a choice between someone who was trying to cram your project into their already tight schedule, or someone who had space and time to devote their attention to it fully - which one would you choose?

Put like that, it's pretty obvious we would choose the person who had the time and attention to give our project the commitment it deserved. But when we're the service provider who's always reaching for that idea of being fully booked out, we don't stop to think of how that affects the clients we're working with.

When the pursuit is more clients, more revenue, more money in the bank, chasing after the ideal of being fully booked out, we lose sight of the fact that we do this because we love our work. It becomes it's own private hamster wheel of hell, because we're always chasing after this ideal that can't be achieved.

When we're fully booked out, we have no control over our schedule. We're hopping from one project to another, in an endless chain that just keeps going ad infinitum. There's no end in sight, no space, and there's no rest for the fully booked out service provider.

We need to rein in our expectations for this term and shy away from it. Because in spite of how appealing it may look, it's glitz and glam is covering up a dark pit of negatives. Negatives we don't see until it's too late, and we have no choice but to follow through or lose the clients we worked so hard to acquire.

How Can We Gain Control of Our Schedule?

The Secret Weapon has full control of their schedule and knows how to maintain it, so they have room for creativity, room for growth, and room to give each project they say yes to the attention it deserves. We don't say yes to everything that comes our way, and we don't chase after the ideal of being fully booked out. Because we know that not only is it hard on us, but it's not fair to our clients.

The first step is to sever our ties with the word yes.

I don't mean we're never going to say yes to projects. Or we're never going to bid or take discovery calls from now on (that would be a bit crazy pants.) But rather, we're going to have to sever our emotional attachment to the word yes so we can instead focus on our schedule and fill it in a way that makes the most sense to us. This ensures we're around long enough to have a schedule in the first place.

From now on, instead of yes, you will say, "let me check my schedule." Even if you're 100% sure you have the capacity to take on the project. Even if you're sure you'll be able to deliver great results for the client. Even if you're in the middle of a dry spell and you need the client right now (especially if you need the client right now.)

Because yes is a slippery slope, and the more we use it, the more it becomes a habit. We want to replace that habit with one that's healthier - checking our schedule, and being intentional with our work in a way so we maintain control, and manage our time and space the best way possible.

Managing Your Schedule

Once we get in the habit of constantly checking our schedule and keeping it at the top of our minds, it gets easier to manage. Awareness is the crucial first part of making sure we don't have too much on our plate, and ensuring we give ourselves that coveted space to give our full attention to any new and existing projects.

But the term "managing your schedule" is kind of abstract, right? How exactly do we manage our schedule in a way that we can see at a glance how busy we are today, this week, next week, and next month?

There are a few methods I've used in the past, and I'm going to go over them here for you. In reality, though, what works for me might not work for you, so we need to keep these three main considerations in mind when we put in place a schedule management system, or method for ourselves.

1. It needs to be easy to read at a glance.
2. It needs to be easy to manage.
3. It needs to take into account our entire life, not just our work schedule.

Let's examine these a bit further, shall we?

Easy to Read at a Glance

I have been a huge fan of paper planners for the longest time. No matter how many apps I use, or online tools I find and try out, I always seem to go back to a paper planner for my to-dos, lists, and notes. There's just something so satisfying for me to write it down, and get it out of my head into a format I can easily read anywhere.

At one point, I was using a paper planner to track my schedule and project load and it worked okay, but after a few projects, I found that it became a bit of a mess to read. Old projects had been completed, and new ones added at a rate that the few pages I allotted in my notebook were quickly filled up. Date changes and edits made the pages messy with scratches, scribbles, and notes added in margins.

It ended up being far too hard to read what was going on in my paper schedule, and I would be constantly recreating it on a new page, so I could actually see what was going on in my day to day.

After doing this for a few months, I knew the paper version simply wasn't going to cut it - I spent far too much time trying to decipher the schedule, and figure out where I had openings and gaps in my weeks.

While I'm not saying a paper version won't work for you, you definitely need to keep this in mind when creating your schedule, and create it in a manner so when you look at it, you instantly know your current workload and can make the best decisions based on it.

Easy to Manage

When I first started actively managing my schedule, I went way overboard. I created a system that was a Frankenstein hybrid Gantt chart and calendar, which lived in an app that was notoriously hard to get connected with other systems.

It seemed like the perfect idea at the time. It had separate categories for the types of projects, the types of clients, the work itself, and a whole bunch of other settings which were overly complex for what I needed it to do.

I think I used that system for about two months, before I finally just abandoned it in frustration.

It was far too complex to be useful. For every project, I had to classify the type of project, type of client, color code it to the type of work it was, and then estimate the timeline to the best of my ability the first time, because there was no way to edit it afterwards. There was no room for overlap, and I had to be very particular because I had created a monster when I first set it up.

It might have been fine if I had stuck with it, who knows, but I didn't stick with it because it was too hard to manage. It wasn't flexible in the slightest, and it was almost more work to manage the schedule than it was to work on the actual projects.

Complete scheduling failure on my part. From that experience, I realized that whatever I was using needed to be simple so that I could manage it easily.

Needs to Take Into Account Your Entire Life

When we think of planning out our weeks and months, it's easy to focus entirely on our work schedule and fit the rest around it. I know I did that for quite some time in my own business. Despite creating my business with the intent that I would be staying at home with my little ones, I very often would squeeze them and the other activities in my day in and around my work schedule and project load.

This ended up backfiring more than once when a kid got sick, or a nap time was missed, or an unexpected PD day came up and I would have no time for the work I had rigidly planned into my days.

Even when all things did go right, I was still cramming in my family time in between work sessions, booking calls while I knew the kids would be relatively quiet, and trying to squeeze every last drop out of the day.

And don't even get me started on any sort of me time or self care. It was pretty much full out all day long and hopefully I could get some 'extra' time to do the things that mattered to me most.

It took someone far smarter than I was to point out the error in operating my schedule like this, and looking back I shake my head at the opportunities I missed when I was working like this. Alex Aanderud, (the man who convinced me I needed to write this book in the first place) asked me about what my daily schedule was, and why I felt as if I didn't have enough time to get everything done. My immediate response was that it was because I was overbooked, or because my kids kept me from focusing large spans of time on my projects. But he flipped this narrative around, and instead asked me what was truly important in my day. What made a difference?

After thinking for a few moments, I realized that when I made time for meditation in the morning and had at least 30 minutes before the kids got up to myself, I was calmer and more focused throughout the day.

When I had time in the evenings to sit down and be creative, I was happier and felt like I was making progress on my hobbies. And when my husband and I had some time at the end of the day to talk and reconnect, my marriage felt like it was happy and healthy.

I listed off several other things and Alex said to me, "Why don't you schedule those things first? If family time and meditation and your hobbies are what make you feel like yourself and make your days go smoothly - why aren't they blocked off in your schedule?"

It was so simple. Deceptively simple. But the most powerful things often are, and so I did just that. I blocked off time in my schedule every evening for family time. I made sure every evening I went to bed with enough time to get a good night's sleep and wake up at least an hour before the kids. I banned myself from working late nights, because that was already scheduled for connection time with my husband.

And it made a difference. A huge difference.

Not every day is perfect. Some days I have to work at night to meet a deadline. Some days the kids wake up earlier than expected, and I don't get to meditate. But the act of blocking off these times in my calendar, and fitting my work schedule around them has made the biggest impact on my ability to have a clear picture of my daily workload and commitments.

How can you make sure your calendar is taking into account your other commitments - to your family, your social groups, yourself? Can you make sure these items are on your schedule, so you can take them into account when planning out your project load and availability?

Doing so will make sure you're not just going to work as hard as you can, but rather, making time for the important things in your schedule too.

Creating a Schedule That Works For You

Now you know what we need to take into consideration for creating our schedule, and things to keep in mind to make it more useful, so we can actually use it daily. Now let's examine some tools and methods we can use in the day to day management of it.

Digital Tools

We're digital girls living in a digital world, so it's no surprise there are hundreds of tools and apps we can use to manage our schedule on our phone or computer. I've used a lot of them over the years, and have settled in on my own way of managing my schedule within my current business and project management platform, Dubsado.

What I like about Dubsado is it takes your projected project timelines you set in one area of the tool, and creates a schedule on your main dashboard, so you can see the overlap of how many projects you have going on at once, and when certain projects are set to start and finish.

With this tool, I'm able to see my regular daily schedule with my kid's taekwondo lessons, my calls booked with my clients, and the number of projects I'm working on each week. There are plenty of other platforms like Dubsado, and every year there will be new ones coming out. Finding one that's best for how you work will take a bit of research and trial and error, but it's worth it.

Google Calendar or a built-in computer calendar is another good bet, because it has many of the same features. We're able to schedule in our normalized activities, our meetings and calls, and then create events that span across a time period, so we can see at a glance how many projects you're working on in any given week.

Many service providers I talk to mention they're using their to-do app to manage their schedules, but I caution you against thinking your to-do app is a suitable replacement for this. To-do apps are a common way of tracking your tasks and the individual items that make up a project, but fail to give you the big picture of where those tasks fall into a schedule, and how they pan out in your week to week planning.

Paper Tools

Ah the paper planner, my biggest weakness and my greatest strength. I have gone back and forth between paper based planning and digital planning so many times, it makes my neck hurt. At this point, I've settled somewhere in between the two, with my paper planner being where I store my to-do items and lists for the week, and my project management tool tracking deliverables and my schedule.

There are plenty of great paper planners out there, (too many, have I mentioned I'm a planner junkie?), and the key here is to find one that works for you, and is able to give you the ability to manage your schedule.

For this purpose, whatever paper planner you use needs to have monthly calendars in it, so you can get a high level, one-glance look at your current schedule and workload.

Fortunately, most paper planners have this, so it's up to you to use it consistently in a fashion that works for you, and meets the requirements set out.

There has been a resurgence in simple paper planners, thanks to the popularity of the Bullet Journal method. It seems that wherever you look on Pinterest and Instagram, everyone and their dog has beautiful planners done up in multiple colored markers and washi tape.

For a long time, when I was first devoted to the bullet journal method, (or BuJo as many affectionately call it), I was obsessed with the gorgeous spreads and beautiful ways others were creating these paper masterpieces. But in the end, it distracted me far too much, and I spent more time worrying about whether a page layout was pretty enough, or deciding how I was going to create my section headers for the day.

In the end, I found it far too distracting and opted for more traditional planners already pre-printed with daily, weekly, and monthly sections, so I didn't have to worry so much about how it looked and could focus on using it effectively.

Whether you choose a plain notebook, a pre-printed planner system, or go all out with the washi tape and colored markers, there really is no wrong way to do this, as long as you're able to accurately track your time, know what's going on in any given time period, and are able to use it consistently moving forward.

Be a Control Freak

It's absolutely OK to be a control freak when it comes to your schedule. Making sure we're the ones managing it from day to day, and not being at the mercy of our client's whims or the inevitable crunch of rush projects, does wonders to save our sanity. It gives us the space to be creative, feel less stressed, and make room in our lives for other things just as important.

Transitioning away from the need to be fully booked out is a big first step towards managing our schedule like a Secret Weapon. When we see how being fully booked out is not right for us, and rather detrimental to our business overall, it gets easier and easier to say no. We can say no to rush jobs, too many projects, and feeling as though we need to get more and more clients to fill up the holes in our schedule.

My husband calls me a control freak when it comes to my schedule. He laughs when I have appointments in my calendar for meditation and for painting, but truthfully, if I wasn't as mindful of my time as I am, there would be no time for these important things, and they would consistently get put at the bottom of the list.

When I first started working from home, I was very fast and loose with that schedule and it showed in my long nights, my early mornings, and the time I spent at my desk instead of with my family.

I'm not 100% perfect by any means. There are still some rush projects I say yes to. Still some days where I need to work late at night or on the weekends to make sure I get a project done in time.

But these are now my choice, rather than a matter of circumstance because I said yes to something I shouldn't have. When you plan your schedule using the tips we've talked about here, it puts you firmly in control, and that's the best way for you to make the biggest strides towards the Secret Weapon status you deserve.

TL:DR

- Not being aware of your schedule can lead to the feast and famine cycle we're so familiar with as a service provider.
- Awareness of your schedule, and its cycles, will stop you from panicking during a dry spell and overworking yourself when it gets busy.
- Instead of saying yes or no, you should instead replace that with, "Let me check my schedule" in order to make checking your project load and overall schedule a priority when accepting new projects.
- Being fully booked out is a glamorous term for being stressed to the max with no time for yourself, or room for new and exciting projects. You don't want to be fully booked out.
- There are many ways to manage your own schedule, but whatever method you choose, it needs to:
  1. Be easy to read at a glance.
  2. Be easy to manage.
  3. Take into account your entire life, not just your work schedule.
- Whether you use a paper planner or a digital app, if it meets the above requirements then you're golden.
- Don't be afraid to be a control freak when managing your schedule. Your time is precious, and the only way to get out of the feast and famine cycle is to track it ruthlessly.

CREATING PROCESSES IN OUR BUSINESS

When I was a little girl, my grandfather used to tell me stories about Henry Ford while we putzed around in his garage. While my grandfather wasn't an entrepreneur by any means, (he spent the majority of his life in either the army or sick from advanced emphysema), he did appreciate Henry Ford's ability to streamline and make efficient all the parts of his business when he was first creating and manufacturing the first cars.

To say my grandfather was an organized man was to say that lemons are sour, it was a no-brainer, a given. Anyone who walked into his garage with his organized boxes and systems and containers for everything under the sun - could tell he was an organized person.

I would sit there and listen to his stories - about how Henry Ford would ask his manufacturers to supply him parts in specifically sized crates, crates he would then go on to use as the floorboards in his Model T. Or how he specifically trained his factory workers to do only one thing so that they could do it as efficiently as possible.

The overall meaning behind these stories was how Henry Ford was not only a shrewd and smart businessman, but that he was efficient and had specific processes in place to make his factories and company run as smoothly as possible.

When I got older and started actually thinking about the stories my grandfather told me about Henry Ford and how they would apply to my forays into entrepreneurship and running my own business, I often think about just how hard it must have been for Henry Ford to create all those processes in the first place. Not only was he running a business that was groundbreaking in what they produced, but it was also an entirely new way of manufacturing. He must have had some serious obstacles to overcome along the way!

Now though, all we hear about are his success stories and the life lessons we as business owners can learn from him and what he did. But we often lose sight of the hard work and effort which led him to be one of the most highly referenced business owners of all time.

Many service providers roll their eyes when I talk about Henry Ford, they say "but Gabrielle we're in a totally different line of business, what can a manufacturer teach us about being a better web designer or virtual assistant?" But they're missing the point of the most excellent business models. They're excellent, not because they work only for one type of business, but because they are easily applied to many different situations and can be adjusted to suit your exact needs.

The biggest thing we can learn from Henry Ford is how he created processes and efficient systems to streamline his manufacturing process. And while no, you won't be asking your printer to create business cards in a certain way so you can also use them to heat your office, you can certainly find the things you do over and over again, and create a specific process for it so it can be done the same way each time.

The reason processes are so important in the service industry is that we, as freelancers, contractors, and people who work from project to project, are completely entrenched in our business. We often fall into the trap of thinking we're the only ones who can possibly do a certain thing, and so we overload ourselves and get burnt out far too frequently.

When we create processes in our business, it's the very first step to realizing not only can something be done the same way every time, but we don't have to be the ones to do it. The first step to eventual expansion is to systemize and create processes someone else can pick up and learn, freeing you from doing them yourself.

A Secret Weapon has learned to create processes in their business not from a stance of needing to outline their own tasks but rather from the standpoint of "how do I do this so I can get others to do it for me?"

And this might be years from now, it might never happen. But the act of creating these processes frees something inside ourselves, which allows us to think of growth as a possibility. Not just growth of revenue, but the growth of service, growth of people, and growth of operations.

Processes are integral to growth, and Secret Weapons know how important it is to create them for their business.

What Exactly is a Process?

I could spout what Webster's has to say on the word here, but I think you and I both really know what a process is by definition. It's something we repeat frequently and is done the same way over and over again. A process is a task or project we can break down into specific steps, so we can easily follow those same steps time and time again, without wasted time or energy.

Some people call a process an SOP or Standard Operating Procedure. In my mind, the terms are interchangeable, but I like the word process better because it sounds just a tad more human. A procedure is medical, clinical, and feels robotic to me. A process brings the human element back into it. It helps us to see that an integral part of a process is the person doing it, not the ability for it to be replicated or learned by a machine.

As service providers, we are the ones doing the work. Over time, we've created specific ways of doing tasks which save us time, money or energy - sometimes all three. It's a big part of our job to make sure we can continue to save time, money, and energy by repeating the tasks in the same manner for each client, and each project.

One of the key differentiators between a hired gun and a Secret Weapon is that a Secret Weapon has learned how to get the most out of our time and energy. Over the months and years of working our craft, we've honed it to be as efficient as possible. Making sure we stay efficient on days when we don't have a lot of time or energy is where our processes save us.

What exactly can we create processes for in our business? By knowing what can be put into a process and what can't, we start to get an idea of the processes we can create for our work, so we can reserve our resources for the creative endeavors they're much better suited for.

The Four Questions of Creating Processes

To figure out if a certain task can be put into a process, I like to ask myself four main questions. These questions are a really great starting point to figure out which of your tasks could benefit from a process.

The first question to ask is, "How often do I do this task or project?"

If it's something which occurs fairly regularly (which means we do it at least once a week), then it can be fair to reason we would save a certain amount of accumulated time over the span of say, six months or a year. If the answer is yes, we do this pretty frequently, then we proceed to the next question.

The second question to ask is, "How many steps are involved in this task or project?"

If it's a task where we do one thing each and every week, like checking our budget forecast, or posting a client update via email, or running a simple report, then it's most likely not worth the time to put together a process for it. These one-off actions are much more suited to recurring reminders or items on a to-do list. But if the task or project has multiple steps (the delineator is about five steps), then we should seriously consider creating a process for it.

For example, I have a client who I build multiple funnels for. Each week I run through a process whereby I create snapshots of the statistics for each funnel, export some screenshots, upload all the data into tracking spreadsheet for each funnel, and crunch some numbers. This process does not take a lot of brainpower. But it's one where there are more than five steps for each funnel I track, and it's easy to get distracted while doing it. If I lose my place or forget a vital piece for the final number crunching step and have to go back, then it makes the entire process less efficient, and I get frustrated. Creating a process for this makes it easy to run through, so I know I have everything I need for the final step and there's no back and forth on my part.

The third question to ask is, "Do I need a formal, written process for this?"

There are some tasks or projects that meet the following two questions but don't need to be written down. Either because we've been doing it long enough or it's something very simple that doesn't need an itemized list of actions and steps to complete.

The fourth question to ask is, "Do I see myself handing this off to someone else in the future?"

We all want to think we're going to be doing everything ourselves for the next foreseeable future, but it's an incredibly healthy mindset to be thinking of how we can hand off our tasks to someone else as our business grows. While growth may be a long way away from now, thinking about what we'll eventually hand off to members of a small team or contractors, can help us make shifts in the way we do business to allow for the inevitable growth.

This fourth question also opens us up to the idea that we can eventually run our business and our services from a place of strength. I firmly believe we were not meant to do everything in our business, and while we may not have goals too, or even aspire to be, a CEO of a large company, we definitely don't want to be doing everything ourselves, forever.

Now that we've got some confines on deciding which of our daily tasks and projects could be considered for creating processes for, what about those tasks that are on the edge? What if we have a weekly task that we don't want to do forever, but also has a few steps to it? It meets the criteria of questions 1, 2 and 4 but it's something rather simple, say taking a client's YouTube videos and creating several social posts from it, plus sharing it to their Facebook page.

In instances where it's not clear whether a process is needed or not, then we can ask ourselves the final question "If this task or project isn't done in a specific way, will there be a loss of quality or the potential for something to go wrong?"

In the case of the task above, sharing a client's YouTube video to other social media profiles. It doesn't necessarily need to be done a specific way each time. As long as each part of the task gets done, then the matter is closed, and we can move on. This is something much more suited to a to-do list than a process.

There are some tasks or projects which won't be so cut and dry. In those cases, we should keep tabs on them. Make mental or physical notes to watch as we perform them and take stock as we're doing the task. Sometimes we assume tasks are simple, but when we actually get down to it, they reveal themselves as more complex, and in need of a process. Others we think are complex, but when broken down are more a matter of time and not effort or skill.

Getting Ready to Create Processes

When we have a list of tasks or projects you want to create processes for, we'll then move onto creating the process itself. We'll take that task and dissect it into its many parts, recording every step along the way, until we have an end to end process to follow moving forward.

There are two minds in the creation of processes or SOPs - some like to create them using software specifically designed for this. Tools like ProcessStreet or Lucidchart, while others recommend the old-fashioned way - just open up a text document and write out each step as you go through the task.

Some people prefer to create video walkthroughs to guide them through the process; others write the process in text format, using numbered lists. I've found creating video walkthroughs is a wonderful way if the process is most definitely something you'll be handing off to someone else in the near future. There's just something about video that allows us to better communicate what a person is doing, what buttons they're clicking, and which screen they're on. This cuts down on confusion and miscommunication when you hand a task off to someone else.

If the task is pretty simple, then a text document with a list of steps to take is most certainly sufficient, especially if it's something we don't see ourselves giving to another person for quite some time, or if it's for our own internal means of getting more organized within our business projects.

Whether you use video or text is totally up to you, but it's important that you go into the experience of making processes with a clear mind on how you're going to format and maintain them going forward. We don't have to get to meta in terms of creating a process about making a process, but having a template you use for each one you create, a specific way, or ordering the steps and information, will cut down on the amount of time it takes to create a new process. It also makes it easier for the person using that process in the future to be able to quickly find the information they're looking for.

I've personally set up my own processes in Evernote and have created two templates using the templating features. I have one template for video walkthroughs and one template for text-based processes. Not having to think as I go about creating a new process saves me lots of time.

The key here is using the method we feel the most comfortable with and allows us to grow and expand as we move forward in our business. We don't need to be training ourselves to use a new piece of software, *and* how to create processes at the same time, that completely erases any sort of benefit we'll receive from creating the processes in the first place.

When we start down the path of creating processes, it's important to keep in mind how people are going to be accessing them in the future and how they'll be trying to find what they're looking for. By using tools that are easy to share and setting up categorization structures and systems to make them easy to search and find, we get the most out of the processes we spent so much time creating.

Create Our Processes

Now that we have a good idea of what tasks and projects we work on that would benefit from having process made for them, and we have a pretty good idea of how we'll be formatting and categorizing those processes so we can find them easier later, it's now time to dive in and create them.

I'm sure you know the steps you take to do any given task or project on your to-do list. We're all pretty knowledgeable about what we do and how we do it. So the first step I like to take when creating a process is doing a quick brain dump of the steps *I think* it takes to complete a task. While not the final process, this helps me get an idea of the flow of the task or project, and the structure of the process I'll be creating.

Nine times out of 10 we'll gloss over, forget about, or oversimplify some of the steps in this first pass. This is one of the reasons why creating processes can be so eye-opening. When we know exactly what it takes to do something, we can more properly budget time, expenses, and attention for it, rather than get overwhelmed when it's taking longer than we thought it would.

Once we have a rough guideline for what we're doing - it's time to start doing it. First, I want you to set a stopwatch because all good processes have an estimated time to complete attached to them. As you go through the tasks, just periodically check in on the time it takes you to do it (you might be surprised).

After you start the stopwatch, start the project or task and continue through the steps you wrote down on your rough outline. As you find steps you may have forgotten or nuances you feel are important to put into your process, stop the stopwatch, make a note of them, restart the stopwatch, and continue on your way.

At the end of the task or process, when you're certain you noted down all the steps completely, stop the stopwatch and record the final time it took you to do the task. This time will become your outset time. So, someone who's not 100% confident doing the process and is checking back and forth which steps to take, this will roughly be the time it takes them to complete that process.

This time is important because I like to schedule my tasks using the outset time so that I give myself and the people I work with a buffer for completing their tasks. You want to be aware of the time it takes to do something, but you also don't want to be grossly optimistic or over-schedule yourself to the point where you don't have any breathing room.

Once you have your completed process document, go back through it and note anything you may have left out or used your own personal lingo for. You'd be surprised how often we call a link button or feature something different than what it's correctly named, and this can lead to confusion on the part of someone who's coming into your process for the first time.

Elaborate where you can in your process, add in more descriptions and steps where you feel someone could get confused or easily take the wrong action. Be as descriptive as possible here, because you can never really have too many instructions in a process.

Once you're happy with it, go through it one more time in a trial run, doing the task or project you're describing. Follow your own process, step by step, and make sure it gets you to the desired outcome at the end. As you do this, I'm sure you'll find other pieces you could tweak, or steps you can add that make it more transparent. The aim here is to never take an action in your task or process that isn't accounted for in the list of steps in your process document.

And there you go - you now have a completed, ready to go process you can use to help run your business more efficiently.

Following Processes Day In And Day Out

We have the processes - but are we using them?

One of the critical issues I see with Secret Weapons who take this important step of making processes in their business is that they make them once, and then never touch them again. This kind of defeats the purpose, but it's a very common mistake, and one I made for years before taking my processes seriously.

The reason processes work so well is so we don't get distracted.

In a solo or freelance business, it's just us doing the work right? Some of us may assume we don't really need these processes, we know how to do our work, and we do it well.

But can we do it better?

That's the hallmark of a Secret Weapon - they aim to do things better each time. Whether it's getting more efficient at the task, making the total time to completion less, or it's aiming to outsource or hire for the task - it's about striving to make our work and ourselves better. Knowing this, we need to use our processes day in, and day out, so we get the most benefit from them.

A process sitting in a folder on our Google Drive or in your Evernote isn't doing us any good if it's collecting digital dust. Processes are living and breathing documents, needing to be used and adjusted as we grow our business and the way we work. They're a direct reflection of our skills and methods and need to be viewed as going hand in hand with our work.

There are several ways we can ensure we're using our processes each day in our work and in our client projects. Each way I mention here can be adjusted so that it's easy for you to use and fits into your own workflow.

The first way is to have a linking methodology for your to-do list. Sounds more complicated than it is really.

The best way I saw this implemented was by Clarissa, a Virtual

Assistant who lives in North Virginia. Clarissa has run her VA business out of her home for the last three years, slowing building up a client base in-between running after her two kids and as she puts it, "far too many animals." Clarissa works with accountants for the most part and has built up a solid client base in her state. She helps manage their customer outreach and marketing efforts, as well as a lot of various admin tasks which vary in their details from client to client.

Clarissa created a searchable database for her processes she keeps in a cloud-based program called Airtable. Every time she has a task for a client, she links to her process in her Airtable database so she can bring it up as she's working on it. When she sits down to create her to-do list for the day or week, she quickly grabs the link for her process and enters it as a note into each item she creates in her task manager app (she uses Omnifocus for her tasks and day to day to-dos).

Not only does Clarissa have a process for each of her tasks, but she also has a tagging system so she can differentiate between similar processes for each client. For example, Clarissa runs a monthly sales report for each client, but each client uses a different piece of software for managing their sales and expenses. A few use QuickBooks, one uses an online invoicing program, and several use custom enterprise software built just for accountants. It's the same process essentially - she's running the report for them and identifying the amount of sales, expenses, and other items for each month. But the steps for each client vary depending on what software they're using.

By tagging and creating processes for each one of those tasks, she's better able to organize her processes and can easily find them when she's trying to plan out her day with an eye on efficiency.

When I first heard about Clarissa's method, I have to say I was amazed at how she had made this idea of using processes in her daily tasks as efficient as possible.

Over the years I've developed my own method of using my processes in my day to day, and while it's certainly not as efficient as Clarissa's, I hope you see how there's no right or wrong way to do things.

Resistance to Processes

When I first stumbled onto the concept of creating processes, I scoffed at the idea - what would I need processes for? I'm not a big company with lots of moving departments and pieces, I know what I do, and I do it well, why would I need to write it all down?

This might be exactly what you're thinking right now too - I mean, you're good at what you do right? You know your stuff, and you do great work. But I know that you're a Secret Weapon and Secret Weapons use every technique or strategy they can to make themselves, and their business better. Processes are a key part of that shift from hired gun to Secret Weapon, so I want you to take the concept seriously.

When I first started creating processes, it was because of a course I was taking at the time about how to run a more successful freelance business. I scoffed at it at first, but I made a half-hearted attempt to create them. But once I created them, they sat in a folder, and I never used them. So, what was the point of that? The main power of processes isn't in the creation of them, but the use of them day after day.

A few years ago, this idea really clicked in my head. I was doing work on a website for a client who had a multisite WordPress installation - essentially, many websites using the same installation of WordPress to function, while keeping their individual pages, posts, and identity. At the time, WordPress multisite wasn't as advanced as it is today, and though there were many tasks I could do once and apply to all 27 of the sites in this network, there were many I had to do individually.

27 times.

It was a lot of work. Not difficult, but time-consuming. I created a process for one of the tasks and was surprised by how much time it saved me. That was the day the power of processes really clicked for me. It then started to make sense as to why almost all the efficiency experts were talking about the power of processes in a business. From that day forward, I became pretty religious about making processes for my business using the four questions laid out earlier in this chapter.

I'd like for you to not need that eureka moment in your business. I don't want you to waste time and energy when you could be a streamlined, process-fueled, Secret Weapon who's able to get more done with the time you have. Someone who's able to take on more clients, without extending the number of hours they work. Someone who's able to raise their rates because they're incredibly fast and thorough in the tasks they do for those clients.

Take a look at the tasks and projects you work on daily or weekly in your business and for your clients. Run through the four questions and create a list of tasks and projects which would make for excellent processes. Start creating them. And then use them, over and over again. Reap the rewards of the increased efficiency in your business.

TL:DR

- Processes are incredibly important for a Secret Weapon. It lets them work faster and more efficient, so they can do more work in the time they have or take on more clients without working more hours.
- Decide if creating a process from a task or project is worth it by asking yourself these questions about the task:
    1. How often do I do this task or project?
    2. How many steps are involved in this task or project?
    3. Do I need a formal, written process for this?
    4. Do I see myself handing this off to someone else in the future?
- Based on your answers here, you can tell if you have a good candidate for a formal process in your business.
- Once you have that process, either written or video, make sure you create an easy to reference way of organizing and categorizing them, so that you can easily find the specific process you need.
- Processes are meant to be used, not collected. Make sure you integrate the use of these processes into your day to day. Reference them in your to-do software, keep the window open all the time on your computer - and make it as easy as possible to use them.

GETTING EVERYTHING IN WRITING

"I'm sorry, but I can't pay you."

My heart fell. There was a lump in my throat, and I suddenly felt like the floor was falling out from underneath me.

My best client. The one I thought I would be working with forever. The one I was super excited to work with each and every day. The one who sent me the most unique and challenging projects, and usually paid me good money to do them - was going bankrupt.

I immediately went into a panic state when I realized just how much money he owed me at the time. It was more than $15,000 and at that moment I had my first (and thankfully last) panic attack.

$15,000 I was counting on to pay my rent, feed my family and pay down the debt I had accumulated in the time period I let his invoices slide. When I believed him as he said his clients were taking longer than usual to pay him.

$15,000 I needed.

$15,000 I knew I was never going to see.

This was one of the worst moments while running my business and looking back, seeing how it all played out, and the subsequent fallout that came from it, I know it was 100% preventable.

Not preventable in that I could control his going bankrupt. Not preventable in that I could control his part of the equation. But 100% preventable on my part of the situation getting to the point where I had $15,000 of money owed to me, and being completely blindsided by someone who couldn't pay.

After that conversation, I went back through all my paperwork with him. Did I have any legal ground? Could I be a part of the bankruptcy proceedings? Could I get any of the money that was owed to me?

When I realized what I had done wrong, my heart fell even further because I realized that beside the first two or three projects we had worked on, I didn't have any legal documents, contracts, or anything other than emails to prove he had hired me for the work that was unpaid.

I was completely out of luck.

From a legal standpoint, the only money I was owed was what I could negotiate from him moving forward. With him being locked into legal proceedings with the Canadian Revenue Agency and probably a half dozen other companies he owed money to - what I was owed was probably the smallest on his list.

My mistake here was getting complacent and not having any contracts in place for the projects we were working on together. My mistake was continuing to do the work for him, even though the invoices from four months ago were still unpaid.

I didn't follow the rules and I got burned. Bad.

The lesson I learned from the darkest year in my business - where I had to pull myself out of a hole of my own making - is one that seems so very simple and common sense now:

Get everything in writing. And, follow those written rules like gospel.

A Secret Weapon knows that legal documents aren't there to make everyone feel uncomfortable. They're there to save everyone involved when situations go sideways. They're there to protect the service provider from doing unpaid work, from being treated unfairly, and they're also there to protect the client from a service provider who isn't living up to their end of the bargain.

Contracts, sign offs, and other legal documents used in a service provider's business are there to help a Secret Weapon do the best work possible. They're the safety net that allow us to create without restraint, to provide our best work, and go above and beyond for our clients, because we know they too have agreed to treat us fairly, and are aware of how and why we work the way we do.

It's all spelled out in black and white in the service contracts we use, and it's incredibly important we use these contracts for each and every project - no matter how small or how much we're tempted to just do away with the fine print just this once.

Why Are Contracts So Scary?

Unfortunately, most service providers have to go through a situation like I did for this lesson to really hit home. How about let's make sure you don't have to go through the same situation and learn from my mistakes instead.

For the most part, we're all pretty aware of why contracts are important. I don't think you can be a service provider for very long without running into the issue of using and having contracts in your projects when working with clients.

Yet, despite how important we know them to be, many service providers are still operating without them, or skipping that step in their process without really knowing why.

I know a very skilled and experienced graphic designer named Michelle who has been operating her freelance design business for 12 years out of her home. She's very well known, quite popular amongst the real estate agents in our city, and she loves her business. And yet, the other day when I interviewed her for this book, she said that when it comes to contracts, she's almost never used one!

I was completely gobsmacked, considering she works with an industry pretty well known for their love of paperwork - from the sale of property, to the use of their likeness.

When we started to talk more about why, she explained how when she first started out she had what she thought was a pretty good contract she used regularly. But one day, a client argued with her on a small clause in the contract about Michelle being able to showcase her work online to promote her own business. Since then, she's never felt confident in her contract, so she hasn't used it.

After examining the clause in her contract, (one which by the way I have in mine as well, so pretty standard stuff), she explained that the clause itself was one she had copied and pasted from another contract she found online. After her client argued with her on it, she lost all confidence in the validity of the entire thing.

This is a very common occurrence for service providers. Not being a lawyer, and usually not having the money to pay for a lawyer to create a contract for us, we rely on the ones we find online and hope for the best.

And there's absolutely nothing wrong with that! When you're in the business of providing design services, or creating websites, or offering admin assistance to businesses, the contracts you can find freely available are more often than not, completely fine.

But since we're not comfortable with the legal speak used in most contracts, we're not comfortable standing behind something we don't completely understand.

How do we fix this issue?

The first step is to strip away the legalese that makes us uncomfortable and go from there. There is no law anywhere that states contracts and legal documents have to be written in lawyer-speak. Plain English contracts are completely valid and just as binding as one written with clauses and words that we barely understand.

I thoroughly recommend you do a search for plain English contracts - there are several of them freely available online. When we break down the complicated clauses into phrases anyone can understand, we can be far more comfortable knowing exactly what our contracts are asking our clients to sign, and we can more easily explain it if necessary.

What If My Clients Push Back?

The second issue I find service providers have when it comes to contracts, is they're afraid that asking a client to sign one will scare them off or will be inconvenient when starting a new project.

I thought this way for years, especially when it came to existing clients. As you heard before, it royally screwed me over at one point.

Feeling as though a contract will scare off a client, or take too long, or be unnecessary in the case of a consistent, recurring client is the key factor in those instances when service providers get taken advantage of, or projects go sideways.

Let's examine this in more detail, and flip the tables a bit so you can see that not only are you doing yourself a disservice, but you're also doing your clients a disservice if you don't follow the same steps for each project, including contracts and legal documents, each time.

In this example we'll use my friend Michelle as an example, so we can see how her situation could have played out differently.

Michelle has her contract and she sends it over to her client to sign before they get started. Her client emails back and says, "Clause 3.4 says you can show my documents on your website and in your portfolio, but I don't want you to do that, I'm not signing this as it's worded right now."

In the real-life situation, Michelle sent her back an email saying it's a pretty standard clause for graphic designers, and that if she didn't want her stuff posted online then Michelle wouldn't of course. In the back of her head, Michelle is thinking there's no way this woman's internal house inspection forms are going to be portfolio-worthy items anyway, but of course, isn't going to say that to her almost new client.

But the client pushed back yet again, saying she wouldn't sign it. Michelle didn't know what to do and she really wanted this client, as she worked for one of the largest real estate firms in the city. Michelle wanted to get her foot in the door, so she felt she had no choice and instead said they could do away with the contract for this case, and she promised she wouldn't put the work she did for the client in her portfolio online.

What other options did Michelle have here?

The first option she had was to revise the initial contract in that one clause. There's no law stating a contract can't be altered based on feedback and requests. Since Michelle really didn't have any problems with not showing the client's work in her portfolio, then it wasn't a make it or break it clause.

The second option Michelle had was to create an addendum. If she wanted to keep that contract unchanged, she could create an additional privacy contract that would state she would keep her work for this client private and not display it anywhere.

This is a far cry from feeling as though she didn't have any choice in the matter and leaving her with the bad taste in her mouth, which prevented her from enforcing her contract for all further clients.

Do I Absolutely Need Contracts in My Field?

Short answer? Yes.

Longer answer? Yes, you absolutely do my friend.

Many service providers feel they don't need contracts in their line of work, or that it would be silly to have a customer sign a contract for small jobs or one-off projects.

But in fact, when you're working in a manner which literally has no inherent security (you're taking all the risk here my friend) you need contracts and legal documents more than anyone else.

If there is a case in which money changes hands and an agreed upon outcome has been determined, then you need a contract in place to protect everyone involved. Since this pretty much describes every service business in the world, then it applies to you as well.

But enough harping on why you need contracts and legal documents, let's get to the good stuff - how can you create and use contracts in your business going forward, so you stay safe and are free to do your best work possible?

Using Contracts in Your Business

When we first dive into the world of contracts and legal documents, it's easy to get overwhelmed with the depth and breadth of available clauses, finished documents, and the difference between types and where to use them.

I find the best contracts, the ones you're most comfortable using and best fit the work that you do, are created from a bit of a hodge podge. A clause from here, a clause from there, and some wording from that one. I personally don't think there's anything wrong with that. We need customized documents for our business, not boilerplate ones we don't understand, or may miss a vital part of something we need to protect.

The first step of course is to do some research and some brainstorming. Sit down and think of any less than ideal situations you have run into, or boundaries you feel you need to enforce in your business. Then, write them down and consider putting strict guidelines around them in your contract.

For example, in my contract there is a clause that states all communication absolutely needs to be done via email or a scheduled video call which I can record. With the rise of apps like Messenger and a constant string of DMs and text messages, tasks and requests can be lost in the stream, and I personally don't feel like being available on all these channels for my clients.

I make them initial beside this clause to ensure they understand, and it makes my life a bit less hectic, since I know I can safely ignore everything but email and not miss anything vital.

Think this through a bit, because it'll help you in the long run. Contracts, of course, are living, breathing things and shouldn't ever be set in stone. Making sure you have a solid foundation from the start will certainly help with fewer instances of contract breach on your part or the part of your clients.

If you're interested in hiring a lawyer to create a contract for you, then it certainly would be a good investment, but for the most part, you can get by with some research and time to create your own. A simple language contract might be of interest in you if that aligns with your business and the way you work. Some prefer their contracts stuffed full of legalese, because of the weighted importance clients put on these types of documents, others prefer a straightforward, no nonsense approach. I fall somewhere in the middle. The majority of my initial contract is written in plain language with very little jargon, but there are a few clauses where the technicalities and legal speak aren't avoidable, so I've kept them.

Where Do You Need Legal Documents in Your Process?

We all know about the initial contract when starting projects, but where else in your process could a legal document help you with your projects? When we take a look at most projects, we can see clear lines of separation between phases or groups of tasks, where it would make sense that a sign off or firm separation would benefit both parties. In my business, there are clear delineators between the design phase, the development phase, and the launch phase of most projects I work on.

When I realized for many projects, we were often hopping between the three, I knew there would be a benefit to placing sign off documents in these stages. This way we could clearly transition from one phase to the next, knowing that revisiting the former would result in delays to the latter or extra charges.

If you're in marketing, perhaps a sign-off in between planning and execution phases would be ideal. If you're a virtual assistant, maybe a sign off after they go through your on boarding process, and get you everything you need to do your work properly.

Where the additional legal documents make the most sense in your business most likely varies from industry to industry and project to project, but I'm sure you've got a few great ideas already that will help you in creating those logical pauses and sign off points in your projects.

By sitting down and identifying key milestones in your projects and areas where delineation between phases naturally occur, you can get an idea of where key contracts and legal documents would be beneficial. Everything from sign offs to clearance letters, to strategy or scope documents.

And lastly, most projects could do with a clear sign off agreement at the end. This is one clear step that has made a big difference in my projects in that it signals a clear, "we are done" message to the client and to yourself. You get to send final invoices and make it very clear that any changes afterwards are not covered in the original project. Therefore, you might require extra payment. These final sign off documents have saved me from tons of scope creep and "just one last thing" requests over the years, and I'm sure they'll save you plenty of the same.

Making Your Contracts Easy to Use

When you have your contracts and legal documents planned out and ready to go, it's just a matter of implementing them. There are many ways you can get your legal documents into the hands of your clients and make it so they're easy to use.

Remember fax machines? I know, archaic right? But I'm not going to lie that those machines made contracts and legal documents much easier to handle than the present-day solutions. Print something off, sign it, and fax it back using the same machine. Easy peasy.

Now we live in a paperless world, and we need solutions to make it as easy as a fax machine. Use that as a litmus test when you're examining methods of getting your contracts into the hands of your clients. Is it as easy as a fax machine? Easier? Or is it harder?

Over the years, I've used many platforms for document signing. A

Google search will give you plenty of options, many free, and many paid. From using Adobe Acrobat's built in signature capabilities to a platform such as DocuSign or HelloSign, to using a project management software which has it built in - these platforms will come and go, and you'll find one to suit your needs.

The main thing to keep in mind is that you need to test it from your client's perspective. Running through the process with yourself as a guinea pig, will help to identify any key sticking points which may be roadblocks (or at least be able to be properly explained them to your clients so it doesn't trip them up).

Making these legal documents as easy as possible for your clients to sign and get back to you is the main goal here. Don't give up if one platform may not have what you need, there will certainly be another one out that suits your purposes, and you can use effectively in your business.

After the contracts and legal documents are signed, you also need to ensure they can be easily accessed down the road if you need them. Having a client document repository such as a dedicated folder in each client's file, or an online platform where you can manage them all is a good idea to make sure these documents can be easily referenced and accessed by both you and your clients.

Over the years, I've used several different solutions for this. Everything from a shared Google Drive, or Dropbox folder, to an area on my own website. There are any number of solutions out there you can use with the same end result.

The key is to make sure everything is clearly labeled, easy to find, and easy to access no matter what device you or a client is using. Removing the barriers to these legal documents will allow you to quickly reference them if you need to and gets you into the habit of doing so on a consistent basis as you go through client projects.

Protection Through Foresight

When we talk about contracts and legal documents, there is a clear divide between the two camps of service providers.

Half of them use them on every project in one form or another, and the other half do so inconsistently, or not at all.

The one overarching quality we all have in common is that we know we *should* be using them, and that it's a good idea in theory. The main differentiator separating the half that use them from the half that doesn't seems to be a sense of inconvenience, or fear of doing it wrong.

I know many service providers who will only tackle something if they feel they've done it the right way right off the bat. But I think we can all agree that rarely, if ever, do we do things the right way the first time. From managing projects, to feeding ourselves, practice and consistency is what helps us engrain habits like these, so they become second nature.

What can we do to make sure this becomes habit in every single project we do? The first step is of course to recognize that we do indeed need them, and not in a, "if I don't do this, I'll get in trouble," kind of way. But rather a way we can recognize how much protection this gives both ourselves and our clients.

Because the real intent behind these legal documents isn't to chain ourselves to a set way of doing things, and forever being inflexible in our method. But rather, their superpower is that they protect us and enable us to do our best work without fear of not being paid, changing scopes, constant revisions, or clients who take advantage of us.

In the end, we all want to do our best work possible and continue to serve the clients we love. But we don't get to do that if we're worried about being paid on time or if we have to close our business down because of a legal snafu, because we didn't make sure we covered our asses.

When I went through the situation several years ago of my client not being able to pay me that $15,000, I very narrowly survived. There were several points where I just couldn't think how I was going to get out of the financial situation I was in and was very close to closing down shop and finding a full-time job.

I'm glad in the end that didn't happen, but there are others who aren't so lucky. Ones who did have to find employment elsewhere, or who were caught in client troubles and had no legal recourse, because there was nothing backing them up in the form of documentation or contracts.

I want you to avoid those tricky situations and embrace the contract like the security blanket it is, not one that smothers, but rather one that protects you from the cold.

TL:DR

- Contracts and legal documents are necessary for the safety of both you as the Secret Weapon and your clients.
- Yes. You absolutely need to use contracts and legal documents if you want to stay in business.
- Using contracts and legal documents doesn't have to be scary, and in fact, you can find many plain language documents online that are just as legally binding as the ones filled with jargon.
- Besides an initial contract, where else in your projects could you create legal documents to support you? Perhaps sign offs between phases?
- Make sure your contracts and legal documents are easy for the client to sign, and also for you to use. Test it out yourself to make sure there are no points of friction there.
- Contracts protect both you and your client. They should not be thought of as an inconvenience, but rather a safety net for everyone involved.

PAYING ATTENTION TO OUR FINANCES

In 2015, I sat down and tallied up everything I owed to various credit cards, lines of credit, and financing. It equaled a staggering $60,000. I could not believe I had gotten to a point where I owed more money than most of my major assets were worth. I could no longer say, "Well if it gets that bad, I can always sell the car and pay everything off." Or, "I'm sure I could just switch it over to a lower interest card and save some money there."

I felt truly defeated, and I didn't know how I was going to crawl out of this hole of debt with anything other than divine intervention. My business was doing okay, but nothing to write home about - I was still essentially living paycheck to paycheck, and I couldn't understand how I had gotten this far into debt seemingly overnight.

I cried, I cursed, and I hid from it for a month or two. I was hoping that maybe, just maybe, it would resolve itself.

But it didn't, and that kind of attitude was exactly what had gotten me in this mess in the first place - I hid from my finances and refused to deal with them properly. It was no wonder they had gotten out of control and had gotten to the point of being almost unbearable.

Looking back, I can see how I was able to get into over $60k of debt really easily, and I want you to hear this, so you don't make the same mistake I did. Because my story? It's not one of miraculously making millions of dollars overnight, becoming a champion who slew their debt and is now living the lap of luxury. My story is far more realistic and one that will get far less link clicks and attention. I'm still paying off that debt, and this lesson is one of those that just keeps on giving after you learn it, over and over again.

From Earning Big Coin, to Crushing Debt

When I first started my business, after moving on from my contract at the oil company, I was badly skewed towards the financial reality I'd been living in for the last three years. In those three years, I had cleared roughly $9,000 a month from my contract. Money was not tight, and I had the funds to do basically whatever I wanted. I was used to making that amount of money, so I grossly underestimated what it would take to make the same with fewer clients, and not much of a referral network or reputation.

Those first few months in 2010 after my first son was born, the business expenses I had went on the credit cards. Having been raised by an entrepreneur, I knew the difference between an expense and an investment, and in those first few months I certainly blurred the lines liberally.

Once I realized it had gotten a little out of hand, I dialed everything back and did okay for a few years. Never really thriving, but certainly making ends meet and working very long hours to do so. I paid off a large chunk of the debt, but it lingered. When one of my clients defaulted on over $15,000 worth of payments, it grew even more. It was always there, growing and shrinking, but never by much, staying steady and being a constant source of frustration.

Around mid 2013 was when something changed. I had dreams of making something bigger than myself and started toying with the idea of creating a design and development agency. Being the planner type I am, I knew I needed resources and knowledge I didn't have at the moment, in order to make it work.

So I started heavily investing in myself and the business. I paid a mentor and enrolled in several agency-based trainings which were quite expensive. I spent a large chunk of time working on a business plan, and I slowed down my clients at the time so I could achieve this.

This racked up my debt even faster, and in the end was a wasted investment, because I decided to not go down the route of opening an agency after all when I got pregnant with my second son.

Rather than seeing this as a failure though, I dived into client work and decided the best way was to raise my rates, create some passive income, and then the debt would be sure to go down.

Throughout this whole time, I constantly justified what I was doing. The debt was necessary. It was an investment. I would make it all back and then some one day. It didn't matter what I made this month because next month was going to be better.

But I was lying to myself.

The truth was, I was horrible at managing my money, and I was scared to admit I needed help. My thoughts about my finances were dripping with shame and guilt. My husband was amazing with finances, my extended family all seemed to be totally fine with it, and then there was me. There had to be something wrong with me if I couldn't seem to earn more than I spent on a consistent basis.

I lived with that shame and guilt for far too long. It wasn't until I started working with a coach that I was able to unpack those feelings and realize they were no longer serving me. This started me down the path of figuring out where I was misleading myself, and how to make my financial life better.

Awareness of Our Finances

Hindsight is of course freaking perfect, and looking back I can see exactly where I went wrong in my business finances that put me in such a bad place for so long. These are mistakes I still make to this day, ones I have to constantly guard against. I'd love to tell you I have it all figured out, and I'm 1000% better now, but the truth is financial stuff is tricky, and being a service provider who trades dollars for hours is harder in this online space where the common message we hear is more, more, more.

The first big mistake I made is that I wasn't paying attention to my money. I hid from it. I ignored it, and I would only pay attention to it when I was really hurting or couldn't understand what my money was going. But after I 'fixed' something, I would go right back to ignoring it because it made me feel bad.

This cycle of ignoring, then frantically trying to fix, went on for years and years. It kept me in a steady downward spiral, putting me deeper into debt and farther away from my financial goals.

When we're aware of our finances, we're better able to control our spending and ramp up the acquisition of new projects and clients. We make decisions based on logic rather than emotion. And honestly, it makes us feel in control of our financial situation, which is empowering for a service provider.

Emotions and Your Finances

The second big mistake I made (and will make again I'm sure), is to spend based on my emotions rather than a logical need for something. I have made countless financial decisions based on my mood and on whether something made me feel good. But a true Secret Weapon doesn't make financial decisions based on their mood. They back it up with logical data to support or suspend their buying habits.

We've all had the high that comes from getting a new project or landing a big contract. Then we have that tempting feeling of having all the money in the world and feeling as though you need to reward yourself.

When we fall under this spell, it can be easy to convince ourselves we deserve a reward or can now spend that money on something we've been eyeing up for a while. And don't get me wrong, rewards and big purchases are all well and good in a business. But our emotional state when we make the buying decision makes all the difference in the world.

When I get that lightheaded, spendy feeling now, I know I'm headed into bad territory and rein myself in. I put myself on a spending freeze until it passes.

But becoming aware of that feeling, and how it presents itself in ourselves is a vital part of the awareness portion of our finances. We not only have to be aware of our finances in general, but we have to be brutally and honestly aware of our reaction to it.

It's neither good nor bad, we can't beat ourselves up for feeling that way or make it wrong. But we do need to control our actions when we're feeling that way. Sometimes the feeling can be enough. We don't need to act on it and spend the money, maybe just revel in the feeling for a day or two, and then afterward if that purchase or reward is still a viable option, treat ourselves.

Becoming aware of our emotions around our business finances and how they lead to our spending and financial decisions is a very hard habit to cultivate. I don't know of anyone who is 100% aware of their own emotions around money, and I think for the most part we never will be entirely aware of how our emotions affect us.

But we get better and we make improvements. This is not a once and for all battle where we slay our emotional demons and then rise the conquering hero, never to make that mistake again. This is more like being on a merry go round, where we come around and around to it again and again, and just get better and better each time.

Alex Aanderud, business coach and stellar service provider, talks about how, when we get into repeatable patterns there are two main cycles. As we spiral again and again through the same situations and the same emotions, we can do one of two things - we can spiral up or we can spiral down. Either way, the spiral is still there, but whether you're moving in an upwards trajectory or a downwards trajectory comes from our own personal awareness and how we deal with the situation or emotion presenting itself.

Breaking the habit of a downward spiral is the key to making progress with our emotions around finances. Acknowledging that we'll probably never be perfect, but we will be better will help us maintain an upward spiral.

Focusing Solely on Money Coming in

The third mistake I've made over the years has been to focus almost exclusively on the money coming into my bank accounts, rather than viewing everything in balance.

Service providers do this a lot - we focus entirely on the next new thing coming in. Which new client, which new project, which new invoice payment. This amplifies our tunnel vision when it comes to our finances, so we stop recognizing that there's another part of the equation - where the money is going out.

For too long, I believed as long as I could make more money, I could fix my mistakes and move on. One big win, one big project, one big client would solve my problems. But it never did.

Because while the getting of the new client and the acquiring of the new big payment was certainly a step in the right direction, I then had to spend a certain amount of time fulfilling the client's project, which took away from any other money coming in to keep the financial momentum up.

This viewpoint has been further compounded by a lot of the marketing materials we see online. The focus on making a huge amount of money in a short period of time has been touted left, right, and center, leaving many of us wondering if that is indeed the norm, and we're somehow doing it wrong if we aren't clearing five figure months each and every month.

But when you're a service provider and actively trading your time for dollars, these income claims and promises can be quite damaging to our financial viewpoint and our sense of self-worth. We have a very real cap on the number of hours each day we can actively trade for money. There is limited time, so if you really want to reach beyond, we need to examine other ways of bringing in revenue that isn't tied to our time.

Is it possible to make six figures each month as a service provider? Sure. Provided you have the right skillset, the right experience, the right clients and the right reputation. But the truth is, I'll probably never make that much money from my own services and you probably won't either.

Is it possible to create a passive income stream that isn't solely reliant on you working directly on a project? Absolutely. But the likelihood of you hitting the big time and making enough income from a passive revenue stream to replace your client work is unlikely. Most service providers with passive income still earn the majority of their revenue from active projects and client work.

Pinning our expectations and actions on something which has the least likelihood of occurring is not smart and leads to bad circumstances, like being $60,000 in debt and wondering if just behind the next corner is the job you'll need to take.

There are many areas of our business finances that we need to focus on - we have to look at the big picture, not just the small aspect of the money coming in and the revenue we're making from our client work. To focus solely on the revenue coming in and working all our efforts on increasing that, to the detriment of the other financial factors in our businesses, is shortsighted. We need to examine expenses, we need to examine what we truly need to live, and we need to reign in our financial bad habits before it's too late and we end up in a situation where we're unable to help ourselves.

Examining and Tracking the Big Picture

One of my friends, John Loudon, owns a successful startup web development and design agency in Glasgow, Scotland. Comments John made, when we were just starting out in a small community of service providers in early 2012 started the ball rolling in my own thoughts about making sure we see the big picture of our financial situation.

At the time I too, was focused solely on increasing my money coming in. I was always chasing the next client, and wondering when the next payment was coming in. But he shared his financial spreadsheet in our group that he used to track every single dime he spent both in his business and in his personal life.

It was a glorious spreadsheet and I, of course, took one look at it and thought about how much work it would take to do such a thing, and how something like counting my pennies wouldn't be needed when I was rolling in the big bucks, which were surely just around the corner.

Having a conversation with him about why it was important to not only examine the money coming in, but also the money going out, was a bit of a lightbulb moment for me. Because even though I was doing quite well at the time, I was still strapped for cash, and wondering where all my money was going. I had just landed several large clients and their initial deposit payments were all but gone, leaving me once again with a gaping hole in my bank account where I just knew money *should* have been.

After walking me through how he set it up and what he tracks, I started to do the same thing. I created a spreadsheet and entered all my business expenses and all my personal expenses. I tallied them all up and realized exactly where my money was going - I consistently had almost double the monthly expenses than the money I was making. It was only the three or four good months out of the year which were keeping me barely afloat.

This simple act of tracking my money made a huge difference to me. Seeing my numbers in neat little boxes and rows and using math I absolutely couldn't ignore or exaggerate was humbling, but it was also freeing.

Once I knew where my money was going, I felt more empowered

to take ownership and control the flow in and out more than I was before.

When I asked John about how he knew what expenses to keep and what expenses to get rid of, he very succinctly gave me the most honest and simplest advice I had ever heard, "If you aren't using it every single day, then you don't need it."

I was guilty of having several expensive services I used perhaps once a month, and was consistently purchasing training and courses for skills I felt were important, but in reality, I used rarely, if ever, moving forward.

Once I realized just how little I was using these services, trainings, and memberships, I cut most of them out and immediately saw some relief from my monthly expenses tally.

The act of tracking my money is one I've fought with since then. It's not an easy thing to constantly see what one might determine to be their biggest failure, every week staring them in the face. But I knew if I was ever going to get my money house in order I had to stop hiding under a rock. I made the commitment to track and watch, and make sure I knew where my money was going. This has made the biggest difference in how I approach my finances, because I'm almost never caught unaware when a big expense comes in, or when a month is slower than normal, because I know I've accounted for it in some way and have what I need to thrive in spite of it.

A Secret Weapon makes sure they track their finances, and by being aware of the total financial picture, they're better able to make decisions about where to spend and where to save, when to prepare for lean months, and when to bask in the glory of the flush ones.

When we do this we come away from the, "I just need to make more money" mentality and are able to embrace the whole financial picture of our business. It becomes much less one sided when we know we have complete control over the money going out and can make executive decisions based on what we want to achieve, and our overall goals, rather than just scraping by day to day.

Getting Help With Our Money

I suffer from I-can-do-it-all-by-myselfitis, and it's a condition I've been battling for years. When a situation arises or a predicament occurs, I charge through without a second thought on calling anyone in to help me. And that worked for some time. Until it didn't.

It came to a point in my financial situation where I had to admit I needed help. My debt obviously wasn't going away on its own, and I felt as though I needed someone who knew financial matters better than I. It was very hard to admit I needed that help, but after I bit the bullet and hired my first financial advisor, things started to get much, much better.

It wasn't that my debt magically disappeared overnight, or that he somehow had some rule-bending tricks allowing me to skip over the necessary steps I needed to get my financial train back on the tracks. But it was more a shift in my own attitude and the mindset I had towards my money. I wasn't doing it all alone. I wasn't on my own when it came to this. There was someone there who could help me.

It's okay to not do it all ourselves. It's okay to ask for help.

Having someone in our corner to help us with our business financial matters is important for a service provider. It could be an accountant who we pay a bit extra to each year to get their advice, it could be a financial advisor who can oversee the business and personal aspects of our finances, or it could be a mentor willing to guide us in this area. But we all need some help, because I-can-do-it-by-myselfitis is a degenerative disease and if we don't treat it, it takes away our quality of life pretty darn fast.

There are a few ways we can find help, the first, of course, is to find someone to help us with our finances. But the other method we can use is to follow some proven financial methodologies for our business. There are plenty of ways to run a business' finances, from percentage based, to expense based, to profit based - and each of them has their merits.

The key to these methodologies is they need to be followed, they can't be something you do for a short period of time and then stop, or switch to something else constantly. Finances is the one area of our business where creativity will never serve us well, and once we find a methodology that works, it's easier to just follow the rules and see the changes in our finances.

I've tried two main methodologies in my business finances since I decided to get smarter about my money. The first was a percentage-based approach. For every dollar that came in, I allocated a certain percentage to my business expenses, a certain percentage to myself, a certain percentage for my debt repayment, and a percentage for savings.

It worked pretty well, but when I was following it I always seemed to be robbing Clarence to pay Carl. I took money from savings when I was having a slow month or didn't pay myself enough when the funds were tight. I never truly committed to it as a methodology, and a set of rules over and above the percentage method of splitting my income into categories.

Little did I know at the time, that I had started to put into place a workable system, but I just needed some foundational knowledge to understand what was going on and why managing my money this way was smart.

Enter Profit First.

If you've been around the entrepreneurial community, I'm sure you've heard of the book by Mike Michalowicz - it's a fascinating read for sure and it made financial sense to me in ways other methods or books simple didn't.

Profit First is based on three core principles - the first being we should be designing our business, especially a small service-based business, on the idea that our profit should be the first thing to come out of what we make, not the last. Our business should sustain us, not the other way around.

The second principle is working with percentage-based splitting of revenue to ensure we have money for our operating expenses, our owner's compensation (that's our paycheck), our taxes, and our profit. By splitting revenue into these categories using the percentages allotted, we make sure we have the money to live and work.

The third principle is needing to reduce our operating expenses as much as possible, to the barest minimum amount, because our business needs to be focused entirely on profit first, not operating expenses.

These three principles have shaped the way I view the financials in my business, and the book itself is nothing short of groundbreaking. Up until I read Profit First, I automatically assumed any sort of profit or my own wages came out last, after any expenses or overhead. By shifting the focus to profit, my own compensation first and expenses second, it makes this whole owning a business and getting paid for it a lot more enjoyable knowing I have a steady paycheck coming my way.

In the end, Profit First is just one of many methodologies. I encourage you to research and seek out a method which makes the most sense for you. There are plenty of people I've spoken to who just don't jive with the Profit First way of doing things, or find how it manages different categories too complicated for their needs. And that's totally fine.

But realizing we need a set structure and rules to follow when it comes to our finances is the vital first step. Find one, use it, and then tweak as needed. Don't spend too much time searching for a methodology. Odds are, any system will work fine as long as it's used consistently and adjusted to suit your specific needs. Finding a financial methodology is not constricting in any way, but rather gives you the structural foundation you can use to grow and flourish.

Tools to Track Our Financials

Once we have our mindset in the right place about our finances, we can then take the steps towards managing our financials. Not sticking our heads in the sand and ignoring our financials is the key first step. Finding something to use to track and pay attention to the money coming in and out is the second part and adhering to a financial methodology to run our business finances is the third step.

Hopefully you will have avoided the big mistakes I did and started to do this early, so you aren't also contending with getting out of debt at the same time. But nonetheless, from here on out, we're going to focus on looking forward with our financials, not dwelling on mistakes of the past.

Thankfully, there are lots of resources designed to help service providers and business owners take ownership of their financials and look at them in a new light. This can include easy to use software tools, financial methods of managing and viewing your finances or apps that make money fun. The tools we have at our disposal today are far more advanced and practical than they were even five years ago.

It used to be that in order to stay on top of our finances we had to be somewhat of an accountant or bookkeeper. We needed to use unwieldy software like QuickBooks or go the spreadsheet route like my friend John. But now, there are easy to use platforms which can help us get a big picture look at our finances in a way that makes sense and we are able to take action on.

From You Need a Budget to Wave to Freshbooks, from 17Hats, to Dubsado to many, many others. These platforms have given us tools that we can use on a daily basis to manage our finances with a bit of initial setup time and a process to check them frequently.

Through the recommendation of my own financial advisor, I started using a hybrid tool called Tiller which has allowed me a bit of freedom and simplicity in managing my money and tracking my business financials. This tool is based on Google spreadsheets, but they provide you with ready-made templates that you can connect to your bank accounts so you can track everything from expenses to income, to paying off debt.

Having everything in one place definitely helps. Checking it every week and sometimes every day helps even more. The act of being mindful of where our money comes in and how it gets spent is important to get a handle on our business finances. While it may seem like the most basic pieces of advice, it is by far the most powerful.

Once we have a tool we like and seems to work with the methodology we're using, we need to work with it for it to work for us.

Committing to Managing Our Finances

Commitment, some of us love it, some of us shy away. But being committed to our finances means we're in it for the long-haul baby. This means setting up a weekly task to go into our tool and do any tracking or maintenance needed. We categorize transactions, run a report to see how much we brought in versus money spent, and we can make sure there is nothing happening with our money to surprise us down the road.

The act of making this a weekly task was something I fought for a long time. I knew it was the right thing to do, and I saw improvements when I actively did it, but making myself do it was another animal entirely. Eventually, I found a way that helps - planning a financial coffee date with myself.

Twice a month I take myself to Starbucks and get a venti dirty chai latte with vanilla syrup. I sit down with my laptop and review my financials, go over my numbers, and make sure I'm aware of what's going on with my money. This twice a mont coffee date lets me take a step away from my office, where I'm inclined to just dive into client work whenever I can, and rewards me when I do it, (working from home has a lot so perks, but fancy coffee isn't really one of them).

How can you make sure you commit to viewing, tracking, and managing your financials on a frequent basis? Can you schedule it in your calendar right now? Can you take yourself out for coffee once a week?

Put it in your calendar and start doing this consistently. The commitment will help you see the effects of managing your financials, and the weekly schedule is just right to make sure you're keeping tabs on things without being too nit-picky and ensuring that you're not stressing out about every little purchase or expense in your accounts.

It took me a long time to get a handle on my finances and start making upward progress rather than downward. But over the last few years, I've been seeing some very positive changes, and it gives me hope that if someone like me, who is stubborn and easily convinced of her own infallibility - then it's absolutely possible for anyone to get a handle on their money and see improvements as well.

For too many years I kept my head in the sand, ignoring the very real danger of my financial world burning around me. But once I looked up and realized there was, in fact, a fire extinguisher close by, things started to fall into place.

This isn't a rags to riches or overcoming demons kind of story, it's more of a "learning painful lessons and wanting you to avoid them," kind of story. Truth is, these lessons are ones I'm still learning. I'm still in the thick of taking action against my debt, and working towards a healthier financial reality for myself and my business.

I can't say I've 'fixed' the problem and am now in the clear on the other side, but I can definitely show you where I went wrong and the steps I've taken that helped me get closer to the ideal end result of running a profitable and financially healthy business.

TL:DR

- Secret Weapons don't stick their heads in the sand when it comes to the financial matters of their business.
- Managing our money is a vital part of being a successful service provider.
- Awareness of what is happening in our finances is the first key step. We need to be aware of what is coming in and what is going out.
- Emotional stability, and not spending or saving based on our emotions, will help to curtail extra spending, and avoid depressing panic attacks.
- Find help from a financial professional if you can, this outside perspective can give fresh light on what can seem hopeless to you.
- Research financial methodologies that you can put in place in your business. I love Profit First, but there are plenty out there that are valid and helpful.
- Track your finances using money tools so that you're aware of every dollar coming in and out.
- Make managing your money a regular thing by setting up a financial date with yourself or putting the task in your calendar. Make sure you do not ignore your finances.

A SECRET WEAPON DOES GREAT WORK

We all want to do great work. We all want to be praised for the quality and craftsmanship of the projects we work on, to be recognized for the effort and skill we put into the products and creations of our clients. But we all know everything we create can't be great.

Every project we work on can't be award winning, and every task we do doesn't necessarily allow us to use the full expanse of our expertise.

In my years of working for clients, I've had my fair share of groundbreaking projects - like the network of websites which spanned across the entire country of Canada, bringing new mothers the resources and connections to bring order to the chaos of raising healthy children. But I've also had more than my fair share of mundane, less than thrilling, boring, work.

It's easy to pin all our hopes and dreams on the exciting work, but in reality, the bulk of our legacy and the majority of the work we do each and every day is most certainly not of the exciting variety.

Many providers I've talked to over the years lament this, saying it wasn't what they signed up for, and they were meant to work on the big things - the projects to create change and make waves in the industry. But in my experience, for every wave-making project, there are thousands of projects that may seem boring in comparison, but will certainly keep the lights on and the kids fed.

So how then, do we balance the exceptional work with the

mundane? How do we make sure each task we complete, each small thing, gives us the same amount of pride and meaning as the big things?

The most important part of the equation we need to focus on then, is the part you can control. We certainly can't control whether a project will impact millions or if it will win awards or acclaim or even if we'll get recognized for the work we do on it. But we can control the effort, the ideas and the way we work within each and every project. That's what we need to focus on - the effort, not the end result.

In many goal setting and consulting industries, they talk about the difference between lead metrics and lag metrics. It's a perfect illustration for what we're going to focus on in this section of the journey to becoming a Secret Weapon for our clients.

A lead metric talks about the effort, tasks, or process that gets followed each and every day. This is something we can control. A lag metric talks about the end results and is something we can't control.

An example of this would be in writing this book. I created several lead metrics I could 100% control. I could show up every day at my computer and write. I could have my software open at the end of the previous day, so there was no friction to writing in the morning. I could make sure I did research for every chapter of this book. I could sit down and write.

These are all the things I have 100% control over. Whereas the lag metrics, things like having a book that becomes a bestseller, or having a book that sells a certain number of copies or makes me a specific amount of money - are all lag metrics. I have no direct control over those at all.

Let's look at this another way. Let's say you have a client who wants to make a certain amount of money each month, based on your input into their social media management. Angela of the Knitters Corner wants to sell at least $5000 of her knitting patterns each month and sell out her two in-person knitting events each quarter.

As her social media manager, what type of goals do you think these are? You'd be correct in guessing they're lag metrics. These are things you have absolutely no control over. Will Angela sell $5000 of her knitting patterns? Who knows? But there are ways you can take a lag metric and create lead goals.

You can post to her social media channels every day, promoting her knitting patterns. You can reach out to influential knitters and give them a sample pattern they can try and promote to their followers. You can create a detailed tracking system to make sure you and Angela are spending her advertising dollars wisely. You can create a number of tasks and projects designed to raise awareness of her in-person events.

All of the above are lead metrics. And lead metrics are what the Secret Weapon focuses on in order to do their best work.

You can make sure the social media posts are exceptionally written, with absolutely no typos. You can make sure each of the influencers you reach out to have been researched, so you know they're a great fit. You can make sure the tracking report you create is accurate and pulls the most up to date info, so there's no second guessing on your client's part.

All of these things you have direct control over. And you can can get better at them. You can become more skilled at lead metrics and goals.

In comparison, lag metrics, things like revenue dollars, follower count, and tickets sold, are not something you can get better at intentionally. But here's the cool thing. Lag metrics will invariably follow the lead metrics. When we focus on our lead metrics, the lag metrics tend to follow suit. They're just not directly tied to one another.

A Secret Weapon doesn't focus on the lag metrics, they focus on their lead metrics, and in so doing, becomes a key player in the growth of their client's businesses and greatly hone their craft over time. Much more so than the hired gun who focus on the lag metrics and gets frustrated when they can't control them time after time, or deliver on promises they mistakenly make.

In this chapter, we're going to go over several topics to help you hone your skills and become much more powerful when it comes to setting and achieving, the lead metrics for your client's projects. You'll start talking in the language of lead not lag, and bring your clients over to the lead side with you, (it's like the dark side, and we definitely have cookies).

BEING INVESTED IN THE OUTCOME

"Yeah, that's not my problem."

She hung up the phone on me and I was shaking. I was so enraged.

I was furious this woman had left me high and dry on a project, because she felt as though what I was asking her for was not her responsibility, even though she could have easily done it in less than five minutes. I now had to work through the night to meet a looming deadline and wouldn't have the one thing which could have saved me hours of work.

This happened in late 2013, and I remember it so clearly. I was subcontracting for a communications and media company who had a large number of people working on their client's marketing and sales materials. The project was relatively simple. I had to create a thirty-page website for a real estate firm with some advanced functionality and I was doing some really great work on it. I was pretty freaking proud of what I had come up with so far.

The last part of the job was coming up, and it entailed me entering over 150 entries into the property database section of the website. I had used some really nice effects on the gallery views, and I was excited to see them in action with their real life data.

I had been told the client company had paid the media company to create this database, and they had it in an easy to use format I could use to simply import the data into the site - easy peasy, lemon squeezy.

So I called the lady who was in charge of creating the database and asked her excitedly if she could send me the file so I could import it, and we could show the client the next day.

We talked a bit about how she had created the database, and we eventually figured out she had used an archaic piece of software which unfortunately, wasn't compatible with any sort of formats I needed it in. After more back and forth, I came up with a pretty good solution, it involved a different software as a go-between, where we could import the original file she created and then export a version I could use in my database.

She became increasingly agitated as I went through the process with her and outlined the steps she'd have to do, (in reality it should have taken her no more than 15 or 20 minutes). At the end, she huffed and puffed about how this sort of stuff wasn't her job and she was strictly data entry, not data export.

No matter how much I tried to convince her it would be simple and I couldn't do my part of the job easily without this file, she just wouldn't listen. Excuse after excuse came from her mouth, until eventually she just shut me down completely, saying it wasn't her problem and hung up on me.

I was shaking with fury when I put the phone down.

How could she not see that by refusing to do this small amount of work, she was making me re-enter all of those property listings myself, essentially redoing the entire portion of the project that was her job - all because she had a narrow view of what was and wasn't her responsibility.

Frustrated and angry, I sat down to start entering the info myself, and ended up doing data entry for the next 6 hours so I could get the site ready to show the client the next day.

This experience is the most memorable for me, reflecting back on times I worked with service providers who weren't fully invested in the outcome of their projects.

The main difference between a Secret Weapon and a hired gun is that the Secret Weapon is fully invested in the end result, the outcome of the project, and will do whatever it takes to get there.

It's a big mindset shift from just doing the work and washing your hands of it when you're done - to riding out the entirety of the project, and making sure your part of things goes smoothly, no matter what is involved.

I first heard this concept put into words by Trivinia Barber of Priority VA, she calls it, "owning the outcome" and as a former Virtual Assistant to some very big names in the online entrepreneurial space, she knows all about how contractors or service providers can develop tunnel vision when it comes to their specific tasks and responsibilities.

When you're invested in the outcome, or when you own the outcome, as Trivinia calls it, you're much more involved in the strategy and the *why* of what you're doing, rather than blindly following a scope of work or a list of tasks. When a service provider is more aware of the overall strategy and end goals a client wants for their project, they're better able to put on their expert hat and suggest improvements, changes, or tweaks to get that end result faster, easier, or with a smaller budget.

When a Secret Weapon steps up to the plate and is completely invested in the end result of a project, it frees them to state their opinions, and reiterate their expertise. We know our stuff, that's why they're hiring us. And when we own that and fully step into that role, it frees us to speak our mind and bring our full set of skills to the table.

Escaping the Hired Gun Mentality

The sad truth is, for many years I operated with the mindset of a hired gun. I was there to do a job, do it well, and then get the hell out of there. The constant search for new clients was my entire world, because I hadn't yet realized the shift in mindset that stepping into Secret Weapon status requires. And that's exactly how the majority of service providers work these days. They do the one job they're hired to do, close out the project, and hop to the next thing, never going beyond the original scope of work.

They mistakenly believe the client, who wants this specific end goal, knows exactly what it takes to get there. But that viewpoint can often lead us astray. A client comes to us because they want the end result, not the specific project.

I'll say that again - **they want the result, not the project.**

A client asking for social media management isn't looking for someone to post for her each day. She wants a larger, engaged following who she can count on to purchase her products or services. They assume social media management is how they'll get there.

A client asking for a new website isn't needing a website. They want more leads for their business. They believe a website is the vehicle that will get them those leads.

A Secret Weapon knows how to dig deep to get to the reasoning behind the initial scope of work. They ask questions, they get involved, and they don't worry about being too invasive at the beginning of working with a new client, because these types of questions are going to get them the info they need to do their job properly - getting that client their end result.

When a service provider doesn't adopt the mindset of being invested in the outcome, all sorts of things can go wrong. The worst of which is we will do exactly what they tell us to do, and it does not get them what they really want.

For a hired gun, this doesn't matter - whether the project or work they do succeeds or fails in the long run is of no concern to them, they did their part, and now they're clocking out.

A client who's looking for a specific outcome and doesn't receive it, no matter the reasoning behind why, will most likely never work with us again. They'll make vague excuses to themselves as to why they won't come back such as, "our styles didn't align," or "she wasn't a good fit," or my favorite, "I'm going in a different direction."

But the real truth underneath it all, is that the end result wasn't achieved and they're disappointed.

It's harsh, because we could have done exactly what they wanted, exactly to the letter. We could have even gone over and above and delivered more than we agreed to. And it still wouldn't be enough. Because the client's goal and what they asked us for were different.

When we're not invested in the outcome, this leads to the wrong execution, the wrong delivery, or even the wrong project entirely for what the client wants to achieve.

Go From Expense to Investment

The other half of owning the outcome of your client projects is we become an investment for our clients, not an expense. Most clients see us as an expense. We're a necessary thing to get the end result they want, but if they could possibly get what they wanted without us, we'd be the first thing to be cut.

It hurts.

Because I know that just like me, you truly want to see your clients do well, (even if it's just for the glowing testimonials or case studies), and the thought of being expendable certainly isn't a check in the positive column for our self-esteem.

But the bonus of making our clients view us as an investment falls to us, it's not the client's job to see us that way from the beginning, it's our job to make them see. We do this by guiding the process of working with us in such a way that we properly communicate to them we are, in fact, invested in the outcome of the project, and want to make sure we do everything we can to get them what they really want.

When you're able to show up and tell them what they might not want to hear then you're on the right path. When you're brave enough to tell them that if they want result X, then they shouldn't do project Y, that's when they start to see you in a different light. They feel supported and understood. Our effort up front to understand what they truly want elevates us from expense to investment, because they know we're working towards the same goal they are, not just doing what we're told.

One side benefit of this mindset shift is that we don't experience as much customer churn as a hired gun does, and our clients stick with us for the long haul. We don't have to worry about being told we're just not the right fit, or that our styles don't match. Because our style and the way we fit is perfectly aligned with what the client wants to achieve.

This helps the client feel supported and ready to invest in us, and it helps us move away from the constant client hustle a hired gun is locked into - always needing more and more clients to fill the queue, because they can't count on their existing clients coming back to them. We break the cycle, simply by shifting our focus from the project to the outcome.

Shifting to Being Invested

I've mentioned how shifting from a hired gun to a Secret Weapon takes more mindset than anything else. And in this aspect, it's more apparent than any of the other topics I've talked about so far. When we identify as a Secret Weapon, when we truly see ourselves as invested in the outcome of our client's projects, and when we're ready to view ourselves as the investment and not an expense, then we're ready to take the actions necessary to back that up.

Taking responsibility for achieving the end results our client wants is the hardest part. A hired gun is one who wipes their hands and says something along the lines of, "not my problem," if what they created doesn't achieve the end goals. But when we become a Secret Weapon, we need to realize this IS our problem, and it is our responsibility for helping the client achieve their end result.

A quick little note here, because I've had lots of conversations with service providers who thought they did what we're talking about here. They believe they invested in the outcome, but some of the items or tasks to achieve the goal weren't in their wheelhouse or perhaps weren't their responsibility.

And I can absolutely sympathize, so we'll examine how you can both invest in the outcome, but not be stuck in a trap if someone else doesn't live up to their end of the deal.

When I was primarily creating websites, back in about 2012, I worked with a wonderful woman who had a sustainable, give-back model jewelry company. She purchased jewelry made by low income women in countries such as Thailand and Nigeria. She sold pieces that were absolutely beautiful, and helped these women create incomes for their families, send their children to school, and pay for village necessities like clean water and seeds for crops. These women essentially owned their own business and my client purchased their jewelry at reasonable rates and sold them via her online store to a western market.

I was 1000% behind her mission, her values, and her business model. I even offered her a non-profit discount, because while she technically wasn't a non-profit, her company aligned with those values and I wanted nothing more than to see her, and the women she supported, to succeed.

I poured my heart and soul into the website, and it was absolutely gorgeous. I don't think I've ever been prouder of a site than I was of the one I created for her. It communicated her mission, it spoke of her values, and it showcased the jewelry in ways that for someone who was her ideal client, it was a no-brainer to purchase (and easy to do so!).

We launched the site to much fanfare and there was a great initial reaction. There were articles written about her, and she went on to create a very successful initial sales campaigns based on the new site, and the content she was creating for it.

But then she stopped promoting her business.

She got lost in the weeds of who the products were for, and who her ideal client was. She stopped creating content for her site, and on her social media accounts. It was radio silence from her company for a period of six months after her initial campaign.

After that six months she approached me asking why the sales on her website had fallen off, and what we could do to fix it. I immediately went to her data to see if there was something wrong with the site and noticed there was a drastic decline in people coming to the online store. When she launched, she had an average of 50-100 people visit her site each day and when we spoke six months later, that traffic had dropped to 3-5 per day.

The reasoning behind it was obvious to me, and I tried to explain to her that no matter how great her website was, if people weren't coming to it, it couldn't perform as expected. I tried to show her how she could use some paid advertising or partnership opportunities to increase the traffic, how she could use social media to get more customers and grow her audience. I went over and above giving her a plan to accomplish all this. All she had to do was put in the effort of creating the content and doing the posting, so she could connect to the people who would buy.

But she had excuse after excuse as to why it simply wouldn't work for her. No matter how I phrased it or how I over delivered to help her achieve her end goals, she kept coming back to the fact that somehow it was the website's fault.

I was frustrated, a bit heartbroken, and disappointed that no matter how I tried, I couldn't make her see past her self-imposed limitations. In the end she went out of business. A beautiful business model, helping scores of women around the world and it went under because she didn't want to do the work required to make it succeed.

In this case, I absolutely was invested in the outcome of this project. But no matter how badly I wanted it to succeed, and how much I fought to realize her end goal, there was little reciprocation from the other end.

I assumed I did everything right. But after further reflection I realized I had made some key mistakes at the beginning of the project, which had snowballed into the disappointing end result. Can you think of what I did wrong?

Let's go over some of the practical steps to bring this mindset and practice into your business, and then I'll point out where I went wrong with this client, so you can see how even when we think we've invested in the outcome, we actually may have glossed over some vital steps which led us to a failed project down the road.

Identifying Clear, Specific And Measurable Goals - No Matter How Hard It Is

The first way to change how we approach client projects so we become more invested in the outcome, is to clearly identify the goals of the project. No matter how hard it can be, or how vague our client is in the beginning.

How many times have you started to work on a project for a client, and when you ask them about their goals they say: to be successful, or to make money, or to get more followers.

These are not goals, they're wishes.

Drilling down into specific, measurable goals, is where we can be confident about whether or not our skills or final piece of work can actually attain those goals. When we know for certain our client wants to achieve an extra $500 per month in revenue from their website, or they want to build their newsletter by 400 people in the next month - these are specific goals we can define. When we know the specific goals we can say, "Sure! This project can certainly help you achieve that goal," or "No, sorry that goal is not aligned with what this project can actually do for you."

We've all heard of SMART goals, right? And despite how much we all groan a bit when we hear the term, nonetheless, they are incredibly useful when we define and create end goals for any of our projects.

When I was first talking to the lady who owned the ethical jewelry business, she was very vague about her goals. She wanted "to make more money" and to "get the word out" about her company. And while those are good sentiments, there's nothing substantial about those. I couldn't wave a magic wand and know how much money is "more" and what exactly getting the word out actually meant in terms of measurable data.

A good goal is something that is Specific, Measurable, Actionable, Realistic and Time Bound. We need four of the five to get a concrete plan in place for making sure we can remain invested in the outcome of our projects (Homer Simpson might actually have gotten it right when he so famously sang, "SMRT")

As service providers - we take care of the actionable part of the equation, so we need to clearly define the SMRT part of the project's goals, before we can make progress on understanding what we can and cannot provide to achieve it.

The goal needs to be specific. We can't just let them leave it at, "I want to be successful," we need to get them to go deeper into something we can work with. Growing revenue? Perfect. Increasing website sales? Excellent. Decrease site bounce rate? We can work with that.

After we get specific, it then needs to be measurable. How much do they want to increase their revenue by? How many sales per day are they getting on their website right now, and how many more per day do they want? What's their bounce rate currently and how much should we aim to decrease it by? Once we know this, the end result becomes growing revenue by 10%, increasing website sales by 25% or decreasing bounce rate by 37%. Getting much clearer now, aren't we?

Once we get specific and we get measurable, then comes the realistic part - is it possible to achieve these goals with the project they're proposing?

Is increasing their revenue by 50% not going to happen with a website redesign? Can we honestly get our client 10,000 new Instagram followers in 30 days? Do we feel there's no way we can get more than 15 sales per day for their novelty cat harness with their current ad budget?

The realistic portion is where we get to flex our knowledge, instincts, and expertise in what we do. They're coming to us to help them, and we can't do that if we tell them they can achieve an unrealistic goal. Gone are the days where a project fails and we get to say, "well what they wanted was unrealistic in the first place." It's now our job to tell them even before we start that they need to adjust their expectations or realign their outcomes with something more feasible.

Once the first three parts of the SMRT goals are done, we can lock it into place with some timelines. When we say it needs to be time bound, we need to put some guidelines around it in terms of how long it will take to achieve this goal.

The purpose of this is twofold. The first is to make sure we have enough time to actually achieve what we're promising. Will it take us 30 days or 3 months? If the client wants goal A and they want it in 2 months, but we know it will take longer, it's our job to tell them. Perhaps we can adjust their expectations or adjust timelines to suit, but if there is any aspect of that goal which won't fit in a certain timeframe, then now is the time to speak up. We don't want to be frustrated or rushed, feeling as though we don't have enough time. We also don't want our client to feel disappointed when we aren't able to deliver in the time we initially set.

The second purpose is to prevent run-away projects. We know the dangers of scope creep all too well, but we've also experienced time creep. When our client takes forever to get us the materials we need, or the review process took far longer than we allotted for, or we got caught up in another project and pushed this one back. This always leads to the end of the project feeling rushed or us feeling pressure to deliver when the timeline wasn't respected from the beginning.

When we set specific dates to both end of project and the phases within a project, we bring in this time bound nature and can stop the run-away projects which eat up far more time than they should.

When we run through the SMRT process of creating goals for each of our projects, we're able to invest in the outcome. We can clearly tell if we've reached the end goal. And if we're off track, we have a benchmark or goal post to guide us back to where we need to be. When we create goals for each project we're working on, we become known as a service provider that gets results. We can easily create amazing testimonials and case studies, because we have measurable data to work from. And when a new prospect asks if we have experience doing a particular project we can say, "yes, I helped client X achieve Y," and be solid in owning the fact we achieved that for them through our services, and how we are invested in the outcome of our projects.

Visually Map Out The Project or Process

Most people are visual. I'd hazard a guess over 80% of people think better in visual term as opposed to verbally. As an online service provider, it can be tough to put into words what we do outside of the data that results in the projects we work on.

If there is any way we can bring some visual elements to represent the work we'll be doing for our client, we should take the extra effort to do so. I stumbled on this quite by accident when I was creating a complex marketing funnel for one of my clients back in 2015, and just how much better this was able to communicate what I was doing, and how much work went into the project was astounding.

If you have any experience with funnels online, you know there are a lot of moving parts. It can be quite easy to forget to create something, or leave out a key element, if you don't have it properly mapped out. Since this was the biggest funnel I had ever worked on up until that point, I really didn't want to forget anything, or leave anything to the last minute. So I created a visual map, drawing out all the parts of the funnel in great detail, so I could be sure nothing slipped through the cracks.

When I showed it to the client, and explained exactly what portions I was creating and the ones they were responsible for, plus how it all fit together into one big piece, they were floored. It was right there in black and white, and clearly showed how invested in the outcome of this funnel I was.

It also had a lovely side effect in that when it was laid out visually, it was very clear the money I was charging for my portion of this project was well worth it. You can talk about what you'll create in a funnel all damn day, but when you visually map it out, it becomes very plain the amount of work that needs to be put into it. I don't think I've ever had to negotiate a price with a client after presenting the project visually, because the value it brings them is very clearly communicated.

The positive implications from this method works in our favor, because it also lets us better plan our projects. If we create a social media calendar with the number of posts, images, and assets we need to create mapped out visually, there is no second guessing how much work it will be. If we create a visual site map of the website we'll be creating with the features, then we won't forget to allot time for feature X or page Y.

Try it for yourself, and see if mapping out your projects visually helps increase the communication factor of the end results of your projects. Doing so will help you become fully invested in the outcome, because once the project is mapped out, you can see the end result right before you - you just need to start building.

Tie Yourself to The Results, With Blood (Not Really, With Money)

Some think money is the ultimate motivator. While I don't necessarily agree, I do know money can put one hell of a fire under a person's bum when the results of a project are tied to their income.

This idea is a bit novel, outside of any sort of sales-driven position. Not many service providers operate on this type of level, but it's something worth playing around with to see if it works for you.

There have been commission-based salesmen for the last hundred years, and the idea of working on commission in the online service provider space is not one we've dived into, because up until this point, most service providers have operated from a hired gun perspective.

Working on commissions lends itself to the idea that we would be tied to this project in perpetuity, or until we renegotiate a different setup. That irks a hired gun, because they want to move on. But a Secret Weapon is invested in the outcome of a project and works towards being invaluable to their clients. The idea of sticking around is not a bad one, it's the whole point.

What better way to do this then to tie our success to the success of the project we're creating? We could negotiate a percentage of sales, we could negotiate a flat payment amount per number of users or purchases each month, we could even stretch out the initial project fee over several months and get payouts as we hit key performance milestones.

The ways we can do this vary as much as the types of clients and projects we work on. Keeping an open mind as to how we can accomplish this is worth considering. The success of the project equals our success, and the more the client makes, the more we make. It seems like a very fortuitous arrangement, if we can get it right.

The first client I ever did this with was a safety-based company, who created handbooks for various trades in Canada. They did a brisk business for the sale of their printed books and thought that getting their materials in an app form would be a good idea, to keep up with the times.

In 2011, I created the first version of their Pipefitter Handbook app, and in 2019, that client is still with me. We negotiated a profit split, and every month I keep 50% of all app sales he has.

Is it a crazy amount of money? No. The apps are definitely a very narrow target market, but it certainly has more than paid for the time I spent creating and updating his apps. Plus, I get a nice little amount every month, which can technically go on forever as long as his apps are for sale in the app store.

Do you think you could institute some sort of profit sharing or commission-based payout schedule with your clients? Or perhaps for certain project types you offer? Examine this idea a bit more and play around with it. When you're tied to the financial outcome of a project, it's much easier to become invested in the outcome. It also has the potential to lead to more profits in the long run, than if you were to just do a per project price.

The Outcomes Are Your Results

When most hired guns finish up a project, they pat themselves on the back and move on to the next one. A Secret Weapon on the other hand, is so invested in the outcome of their projects and determined to help their clients reach their goals, that it becomes a sort of badge of honor when they display the results they get.

Which do you feel would be more enticing to a prospect - if you were to say, "I helped my clients increase sales from their email marketing campaigns by 20% over a period of three months," or "I created email marketing campaigns for my client?"

If I was hiring someone, I would totally go for the former and feel like I had to get more info from the latter.

Having specific, measurable results isn't just fantastic for the projects themselves, they're amazing when you use them in your client testimonials, results showcases, and just plain showing off your skills around town and on social media. The more invested you are in the outcome of the projects you work on, the more likely you are to have these types of amazing success stories and client testimonials.

It's hard for us as service providers to make this switch in our mindset. It requires more up-front work; it takes a bit more effort and forethought to make sure we get these things right in the beginning. But the payoff for this extra effort is amazing success stories, higher satisfaction with the work we do, and clients who keep coming back to us again and again. They come back because we've proven to them we get results, and care for their business success as much as we care about our own.

Examine how you can bring this mindset and way of working into your own business and commit to being invested in the outcome of your client's projects. You'll start seeing a big difference in your business, and soon all your clients will be calling you their Secret Weapon.

TL:DR

- Investing in the outcome is a mindset shift that takes you from hired gun to Secret Weapon by having you truly care about the end results each project you work on achieves.
- When you're invested in the outcome of a project, you become more of an expert regarding the strategy and execution, and less worried about crossing tasks off a list.
- When you invest in the outcome of your projects, you transition your services from expense to investment.
- Taking the time to discover your client's true goals and making sure they are specific, measurable, realistic, and time bound will make it more likely you'll achieve them.
- Visually representing your projects can help you clearly communicate to your client both the scope of work, and helps you plan to achieve the outcomes easier.
- While a bit 'out there,' look into how you can tie yourself financially to the outcome of a project. Whether it's commission based, percentage based, or profit split, when you have money riding on it, it's easier to invest in the outcome of a project.
- When you fully invest in the outcome you get better success stories and your clients come back to you again and again.

AIMING FOR 92%

What do you do when you see a project, social posts, website, or email campaign which was shoddily put together? You probably cringe a bit inside, don't you? I know I do. When things are broken or could have been done so much better, as a Secret Weapon, we immediately think about what we would have done differently to make it more successful, less of an eye sore, or function properly.

The nature of a Secret Weapon is to be on the lookout for things aren't done to our own internal standard. We thrive on our own, ensuring the I's are dotted, and the T's are being crossed. We pour over our own work to make sure it's error free, and tweak until we're satisfied it's finally ready to go to the client for approval.

We take extra time to make sure it's as close to perfect as we can possibly make it. And it shows, because when we decide we're ready for the title of Secret Weapon, it means we hold ourselves accountable to a higher standard of work than a hired gun.

A Secret Weapon aims to achieve 100% in their work, and only calls it quits when they get to 92%.

Why the 'Just Ship it' Mentality Doesn't Apply to Us

There's a very liberating movement out there in online business, and I'm sure you've heard it time and time again:

"Just ship it."

It's good enough, no one else will notice, it's fine and you can be happy with it. There's bound to be mistakes in everything, and you can't find everything, so don't worry - just ship it.

I'm not going to lie - this mentality is super enticing. Who doesn't like the idea of being relaxed about the projects they create, and not worrying so much about the final end result? What counts is you getting it out into the world, right?

I agree, when you're doing work for your own business, perfectionism can rear its head and prevent you from putting out content, launching offers, and selling what you have to people who want it. It's a very real thing for small business owners, and I'm by no means knocking it - the just ship it mentality has its place, and I'll applaud whoever came up with it originally, for its ability to get these people to overcome their perfectionistic tendencies.

But it doesn't apply to Secret Weapons, or service providers of any sort. Just ship it, and the 80% mentality - is not good enough for a Secret Weapon. That's not what we aim for, and we wouldn't ever be happy with it as a final result. We most certainly would never show a client something which was only 80% of the final end result.

No one gives medals for running 80% of a race. You don't get the X-Prize for going 80% to space, and you certainly don't get any dessert if you eat 80% of your dinner (at least in my house).

So why then would we ever get to 80% in our work? Why would we settle for something so clearly ineffective, or falling short of our end goals? Why would we put our name on something we knew we could have gotten at least 12% better with a marginal amount of effort?

I experienced this quite painfully on a project with a client, who we were creating an online course for. Generally, my clients come to me with a clear-cut idea of what they want to teach, how they want to teach it, and have the majority of the content ready to go. We simply have to tweak and adjust for delivery in an online course environment, make sure the student is supported, and has clear learning objectives along the way.

This client had a lot of content, but it was older content, and she made it pretty clear that she would be updating it as we went along to reflect her new modality, and her findings since she first published it.

For some reason - I don't really know why to this day - I created the course rigidly based around her old content, with no real wiggle room to accommodate her new teachings.

If I had taken the time to slow down and investigate, asked questions where needed as to which parts needed updating, and which parts were fine to stay the way they are - I probably would have saved myself tons of wasted time and effort.

I rushed through the project, wanting to get to the other side quickly, so I could collect the remaining deposit. I needed the money, and so I thought that since the client wasn't very tech savvy - I would be able to get away with going about 80% of the way, and maybe tweaking it later as needed.

Oh that ended up biting me in the butt later, since when I sent her the completed course curriculum, with her content neatly placed into models, lessons and engagement elements that would support her learners - she had a bit of a meltdown.

Turns out, the assumptions I made on her content were completely wrong, and the entire curriculum had to be redone. Ouch. The rushing and focus on finishing, rather than on quality, cost me by having to do the project twice.

It's a mistake I won't make again and learning it the hard way certainly cemented it in my mind.

Have you ever sent a project to a client, and knew it just wasn't quite your best work? Say you were short on time, or short on inspiration, or you had too many tasks going on at once, so you figured hey why not - they won't be able to tell the difference anyway?

I'm going to hazard a guess that those projects are the ones which ended up taking much longer, because of revisions and having to go back over the work you rushed and pushed through. And what happened to that client after the fact? Were they a bit leery about working with you? Are you still working with them at all? Or did they go on their way and not become a repeat customer?

Go back and examine your past projects, think of the ones you didn't do your best work on and where you are now with that person. I wouldn't be very surprised if those clients didn't end up sticking around for much longer after you turned in 'good enough' work.

92% Defines a Secret Weapon

What is the one thing Secret Weapons do that hired guns don't? It's a broad question I know, and in this book, you'll find many examples.

But there's one defining feature, one defining behavior I feel Secret Weapons embody that other service providers do not. It's the drive to get a project as near to perfection as possible. They go the extra mile, they take the extra time, (and account for it in their schedules), and they make sure every project they work on is as close to 100% as possible.

I call this behavior the 92% - why 92%? Because it's much easier to strive for 100% and hit 92%, than it is to get to 'good enough' and ship it to the client.

Getting your projects to 92% brings a host of benefits with it, and Secret Weapons who focus their energy on getting a project to that percentile, can expect to see those benefits pretty quickly.

But before I dive into the benefits of this way of working, I want to make a clear distinction between working towards perfection, and perfectionism itself.

A Secret Weapon knows there's no such thing as perfect. As much as we may strive towards it, and hope to attain it, there's simply no reasonable way we can expect ourselves to be perfect or to do perfect work. But we can strive to be as close to it as possible when we dedicate ourselves to working on other people's projects.

Perfectionism is the voice that says, "this isn't good enough, you're not good enough." Perfectionism has boundary issues. A Secret Weapon knows being perfect and doing perfect work are two separate things, and neither of them is possible. One of them is worthy of striving for, but neither of them is truly attainable. Keep an ear open to the voice of perfectionism, and label it as such when you're working on your client projects.

The most powerful method I know of offsetting the tiny voice of perfectionism is pride. Pride gets a bad rap, but it's super useful as the combatant of perfectionism, and a key tool a Secret Weapon uses to help them achieve great things in the work they do. When you have pride in your work, not only does it feel freaking fantastic, but it's also an indicator you've reached that 92% mark. Having pride in the work you do is incredibly healthy as a service provider. Knowing deep down that you do great work helps you to continue to do that great work, day after day, year after year.

And when you have pride in your work, by extension, your clients are proud of the work you do. It's a great big never-ending cycle of awesome. Your clients can see you're proud of your work, and when they see that, they are instantly more confident that your work will help their own business achieve the goals they set out for it.

When we do our best work, work we're proud of, it really shows to our clients. Not only are they happier overall, but they come back to us again, and again, and again. Because they know we're going to do a great job on their projects. When this happens, we keep our current clients. They don't go looking for someone else for the next project - they come right to us first. A Secret Weapon who keeps their clients around longer has a much more stable income than one who doesn't know if a client is ever going to come back again.

The best thing about making a commitment to doing your best work, to reaching that 92% on every single project you work on, is that new clients come to you easier as well.

You get a reputation. A good one.

Your reputation is something which only comes from doing great work time and time again. It's a precious commodity for a Secret Weapon, and we treat it like a dragon treats its gold - something to be hoarded and protected at all costs (fire breath optional). When you commit to reaching 92% in all the work you do, your reputation starts to precede you, and it starts to do the heavy lifting for you when it comes to new clients.

TL:DR

- Secret Weapons have a very high internal standard for the work they do
- The "Just Ship It" mentality does not apply to service providers and while a noble thought, it's not acceptable when you're doing client work
- A Secret Weapon strives to reach 100% and only accepts 92%
- It's not about being perfect, but rather striving for a higher level for the work you do for clients
- Perfectionism says that you're not good enough, but pride says, "yes I am!"
- Using pride as a means to combat perfectionistic tendencies we show up differently and are able to confidently say we do our best work

ASSESSING THE ENTIRE SITUATION

"But that's not my job."

"How was I to know they also used XYZ?"

"If I had known that, I wouldn't have recommended this."

"Oh, well that makes this work not needed then."

All of these are the cries of the hired gun. They come from a place of only worrying about what they were specifically hired to do, never mind how the task or project fits into the landscape of the business, or how it may help or hinder the goals of their clients.

When I was fresh out of college, one of my first jobs was to help run the production line at a printing and silk-screening shop. We created printed products like brochures and business cards, vinyl cut signs, vehicle wraps, and silk-screened hundreds of t-shirts every day.

My job was to do the grunt work for every department. I did a little graphic design, a little production, a little sales, a little marketing - I was all over the place, and essentially just pitched in where I was needed at the time.

There was one week where I learned this lesson hard. We had a busy week, lots of big orders coming in, and the challenge was to schedule them in our printing presses and silk-screening department so they would all get done, on time, and with a reasonable profit margin.

Seemed pretty simple enough for me. I had been doing it for a while now and was up to speed on what the various departments could handle. I confidently told my boss, "I got this" and proceeded to run the show.

But then the phone rang.

One of our best customers, a man who ordered thousands of

dollars' worth of products every month, (and we had been told specifically to serve to our highest capacity), placed a rush order for an upcoming charity golf tournament he was hosting. It was a big job - several hundred t-shirts, a bunch of printed materials, and several big signs to put up on the golf course as the potential donors swung their clubs to raise awareness for diabetes research.

Of course, I said yes.

We were told explicitly to serve him in whatever way we could and saying no to this order meant blowing our previous month's revenue out of the water. I eagerly said yes and told him we'd have it all for him by the due date.

But I royally screwed up.

I forgot to take a moment and assess our current situation, our current workload, and the people involved in getting these orders completed.

It was the middle of summer, so many of our employees were taking vacations and spending time off with their families, (summer in Canada is precious, so no one messes with another's vacay time).

I took the order back to the boss and proudly showed him what I had just closed, expecting him to be excited for the incoming revenue, and the chance to sponsor such a high-profile event.

He was furious.

I was a bit taken aback at first - how could I have possibly screwed this up? I mean, the order was big, he was our best client, and the chance to put our logo on these materials was a big boost to our advertising budget (i.e. non-existent at that point).

My boss couldn't believe I had agreed to do this with the upcoming week we had before us. We had three employees gone, and the departments were running at max capacity for the next three days. Even if we could fit this stuff in, we couldn't do so until two days before I had promised him we'd get him the order completed.

On top of that, the product we needed to make the signs usually took 3 business days to be delivered, so we'd literally get it the day before the signs were due. Plus our usual supplier for the special glow in the dark silk screening ink he wanted on the t-shirts had just gone out of business, and we hadn't sourced a new supplier for it yet.

I hadn't assessed the entire situation.

It was a complete nightmare, and we were a bit screwed because of it.

Fortunately for me, (and my love of being employed), we managed to pull it off. I worked several double shifts, filling in for the employees who were on vacation, (my mess, my cleanup), and we outsourced part of the order to another shop who had the capacity at the time.

I spent three whole days at the shop, going home periodically to shower, eat, and catch a few hours of sleep, before returning to complete various parts of the order. I bribed the supplier for the sign material to let me come pick it up, and saved us a day and a half for shipping. I spent three whole hours sourcing a new supplier for the glow in the dark silk-screening ink, so I could go and pick that up as well.

It was the most intense three days of my life, and I still can't believe I was so stupid to put myself in the situation in the first place.

When I was done with the order and everything was shipped off to the customer, (who was incredibly happy with everything by the way), I turned to my boss, expecting a pat on the back and three cheers from everyone there for pulling it off.

He glared at me.

"If you ever do that again, you *will* be fired Gabby, I don't care if you can pull it off or not, that's not how we run this show." He turned, walked back to his office and slammed the door.

And I totally deserved it.

Hired Guns Don't Worry About the Entire Situation

Many service providers act exactly how I did back in that print shop - they look for the quick win, the one-off project, and they don't worry about how it fits into the landscape of the entire business. This can cause untold issues and disastrous results if they miss a key element, or don't assess the entire situation properly.

When you have the mentality of a hired gun, you're focused 100% on what the specific tasks of a project are, and don't worry, or care, about how this may affect other items in the landscape. I've heard many horror stories about a provider hired to do a project, but didn't take into account how systems were connected, how a business ran their setup, or even what the specific end goal was.

This type of mentality can cost a client, not only the amount of money they paid us, but has the potential to have far reaching complications that extend to many other parts of their business. If I had to guess right now, I would say conservatively speaking, this type of mentality and way of working has cost the average business owner thousands of dollars a year. Not only in sunk costs paying for the provider's work, but also the aftereffects which leach into many other areas of their business.

Take for example my friend Dianne. She had hired a virtual assistant to manage her online booking system. Dianne runs a nurse-for-hire service, which allows nursing homes, clinics, and individuals to hire a trained and licensed nurse to come to their home or business for part time or contract work.

Dianne was run ragged trying to coordinate all the bookings, and even though she had a pretty good system for it, it certainly wasn't something she needed to be doing herself, so she wisely decided to outsource it.

The person she ended up hiring seemed reputable enough, she had great recommendations from others, and had the skills Dianne was looking for to do the job and manage the bookings on a part time basis.

About a month after hiring her, Dianne noticed her monthly sales and booking reports were looking a bit… off. She wasn't entirely sure what was wrong with them, but she knew the numbers didn't make sense in terms of what she was seeing in the bank account. There was far more money reported in the sales reports, than was showing in her company accounts, and her operations manager was messaging her constantly wondering if they had enough to pay several large upcoming expenses.

Dianne checked in with the person who was managing the booking system and was assured everything was running smoothly, and she had even made some improvements to the system, so it was easier for her to manage and provide the reports.

After another week of not being able to figure this issue out, Dianne went into their booking system to see what the matter could be. And she was absolutely blown away by what she found.

Not only had the woman she had hired turned off several very important reporting features, (because she said they were confusing to her), but she had also disabled a very popular form of payment that her clients used regularly and replaced it with a manual pay option!

She had done all of this without running it by Dianne, and her reasoning behind it was that it saved *her* time, because she didn't have to chase down bookings, which were made but not paid for. She felt as though the manual payments would have been followed up on and then received by the company's bookkeeper or accountant. In the end, the changes this person made left Dianne scrambling for lost revenue, as they had unwittingly been providing services to people without being paid!

If this service provider had simply checked in with the people who had been running the business, she would have discovered the reasoning they did things this way and perhaps had not cost the company she worked with thousands of dollars, and eventually, her job there.

This is a classic case of not assessing the entire situation of a project. It's become quite prevalent in our gig economy of late, where service providers are intent on getting the one-off jobs, and feel as though the extra work of discovering how a particular project fits into the landscape of a business just isn't worth it.

Secret Weapons Take the Time to Understand

Knowing that the project or task you're doing fits into the broader landscape of an entire business is the key difference that separates how a hired gun and a Secret Weapon approach a project. It's not only a different mindset, but it also manifests itself into how a Secret Weapon approaches the setup and the prospecting part of projects and new opportunities.

For the most part, it's all about asking more pointed questions and taking the extra time to discover how the project they're working on fits into the way the business operates.

But how can we do this if we're simply hired for one project or one task, and we don't know the way it fits into the rest of the business? What can we do to figure out the information we need to know in order to not affect other areas of the business? Since the defining feature of a Secret Weapon is that they get asked to do more and more within one business and prove themselves valuable, there's a fine line to walk here between getting the info we need, and seeming as though we're prying into the inner workings of a company when we're just starting out.

So let's examine a few ways we can put this concept into practice into our own way of working with our clients so we avoid causing irreparable damage, (like in the case of Dianne), and we're able to go above and beyond to prove to our new client that we will be an asset that they should hold on to for future work.

Asking the Right Questions

We touched on this in a previous chapter, and how it pertains to when we're first getting a prospect into the client stage. But it doubly applies here as well. After we've secured a project is not the time for the questions to stop - in fact, a good rule of thumb is if we're unsure of how something fits into the grand scheme of things, the best thing we can do is to ask and not make assumptions.

Let's get a bit practical here. Let's say you're a web designer who's been hired by a client to redesign their website. You're super excited, because this is a business you were ecstatic to see land in your inbox. You pulled out all the stops to wow them with your onboarding, quoting, and follow-up sequencing, to make sure they felt supported and comfortable working with you on this project.

Once you got the yes, you did a big ol' happy dance, and after making sure the deposit was in place, you dived right into the design of this new website.

But you're already doing it wrong.

Wait, what? Hold your horses dear, you're probably saying, I know what I'm doing here and I've been developing websites for ages with spectacular results. Sure - you're totally right.

But if you were to take a few moments, and pause before diving into the fun stuff, you'd realize perhaps you should make sure whether there's something worth keeping from the old site. I mean, this company has been around for a while now, haven't they? They have enough money to hire you, and invest in a new website to better showcase themselves, so this means they've been doing something right, correct?

Rather than diving into the fun stuff, a Secret Weapon first examines what's currently working in any given project. We don't advocate the new for newness sake.

Let's apply this to a different example. Say you're a copywriter who's been hired to create compelling email copy for a company's new spring launch of their line of clothing. You'd, of course, go back through their old campaigns to see what worked and what didn't with their existing promotions, correct?

You'd see what tone of voice their audience resonates the most with, (i.e., which previous emails got them sales and which didn't), and what style of email promotions made the company the highest return on investment. By doing this one simple task, (I said simple, not fast), you could save yourself the heartache of delivering something to your client that was either, a) ineffective as it had been tried before or b) totally a waste of investment as it didn't give them a reasonable return.

Whether it's the words used previously, the systems they're currently using or the way they handle their bookkeeping. You need to know these things before you start on the project you're about to dive headfirst into.

Make sure you're asking the right questions as they pertain to what you're doing and you'll save you and your client a lot of wasted time and money.

Simple Situation Assessment

We all want an easy way to keep this in mind for each and every new client and project we start on. Lucky for you, I created one specifically after being the cause of a significant client project meltdown.

In 2012 I was two years into my official business and was working on tons of small and medium-sized projects for local companies and the arts community in my city. It was going really well, and I was at the point where I had a good balance of work and home life, raising my first son who was two at the time and keeping a house, a business, a family, and a marriage pretty well balanced.

It's just at these times when things are going well, we start to take our processes and projects for granted don't we? We think it's okay to cut a few corners or perhaps skip a step here and there, because everything has always worked out in the end before. We become complacent.

I became complacent.

It was springtime, and the weather was turning nicer, the snow was melting, and I had just been hired by a local communications company to create a website for one of their clients, in which, they would supply the design and the content, I just had to build the thing.

It seemed like a great opportunity, I had the chance to prove myself to this agency, and get shortlisted for future projects, of which they had many. So I dived into the website build, knowing they had a short turnaround time and this client of theirs was very anxious to get this up and running.

I did a whirlwind development and turned around the website is a very short time period. Everyone was impressed, and they were all excited that they could get this project up and running ahead of schedule. A few tweaks and changes in the revision period, and I was given the green light to take the website live for the client on their server.

I started the process and started to push the website live. Their old website was built on a custom-made platform that was a bit foreign to me. I had never run into it before, so wasn't 100% positive which folders contained which assets. After contacting the agency with a few questions about several of the folders on the server, I was told the client had a backup and I was fine to overwrite them and get the new site live. So, I did.

Against my own best judgment, and as a clear violation of my own policy at the time, I rushed to get the site live. I didn't do my own backup, and I overwrote the files. The site was live, and I was proud of myself for shining in this test project.

Until the phone rang.

On the other end was a very unhappy agency owner saying their client was complaining a bunch of their supplier assets were missing, and none of their distributors could access their control panel to manage their stock or order new products.

I tried to defend myself, saying the project manager at the agency said none of those folders needed to be saved, and I was just doing what I was told (by the way, whenever we feel as though we were, 'just doing what we were told' it is a great indicator of the hired gun mentality creeping in.)

Deep down, I knew I was in the wrong. I hadn't followed my own protocol. I didn't make a proper backup myself, and I skipped several steps of my own process in order to please a new client I wanted to impress.

Well, I certainly did the opposite of that now, didn't I?

If I had taken the time to slow down and follow my own process, I would have done my due diligence and asked the right questions to make sure I wasn't overwriting anything important on their server. I would have made sure I created a proper backup, and I most certainly would have gotten everything the client said and approved in writing, to make sure I had a paper trail to prove who asked and who ordered what, to ensure I could go back to it when I needed it.

Very hard lesson learned.

In the end, I managed to salvage their old site and the distributor portal, but not after a lot of headaches and a very late night, fixing the things I had broken in my haste.

After that night, I vowed never to do that again, and though I may have had some hiccups here and there since then, I can honestly say I haven't screwed up that bad again.

The aftermath of that project was what birthed my action checklist to ensure every action I take on a project is well informed, and that I've properly assessed the situation. Using these three questions before you take action on any specific project or task will make sure you avoid the headache I went through on that fateful project so many years ago, and hopefully save you a few late nights fixing a mistake, which never should have happened in the first place.

The Three Questions

In order to make sure we have the info we need to proceed for any given project, we need to ask these three questions. These are the precursor questions, which sometimes leads to straightforward answers, and other times leads us to other, more appropriate questions in order to get the entire situation figured out before proceeding.

Many times, these questions have not only saved my bacon, but they've uncovered issues and roadblocks which weren't apparent in the beginning. They've saved me countless hours of frustration, and from having to contact a client with my head hung in shame after making a mistake. Usually a mistake I could have avoided if I had only asked these questions ahead of time. Let's examine these three questions, so you can use them in your business moving forward.

Question #1: What areas of their business does this project affect?

This can be misleading, because many times, an initial project scope or proposal can seem straightforward, but in the end, it touches multiple parts of a client's business. In the case of the client, where I accidentally overwrote their distributor management portal, the website project, in fact, touched another part of their business I was entirely unaware of.

Follow-up portions of this question could be:

1. What other platforms does this project need to use or will it affect?

While many projects seem straightforward, we all know business can be interwoven and tricky to untangle. Do they need to integrate with other systems? Does the project need to borrow or use parts of another system or platform? Will the changes in what we're working on affect how they use another platform?

2. What departments have stakes in this project?

While we'd love to only have one touchpoint for every project we create, the truth is that there are often many different departments or stakeholders in any given project or task. An accounting-based project could touch their client acquisition department. A marketing project could also include their admin department. Making sure we know everyone who's involved and may be affected, is key to making sure our project doesn't adversely affect those other parties.

Question #2: What came before and why did it not work?

Being hired to do a certain task or project is one thing, but having the entire scope of what has been done before and why it didn't work, is crucial to us avoiding those same missteps.

If we're being hired to do a client's marketing, then why did their previous marketing not work? What did they try and what were the results of it? If our project is to create a new way for clients to contact them, what were they using before, and what issues did they have with that method?

Follow-up questions to this could be:

1. How did they know this past endeavor didn't work? What feedback or data do they have that indicates it wasn't effective?

We want to make sure we're not acting on gut instincts or a desire to do something different for different sakes. Asking for the data or personal stories by the people who have been affected or have used the past project is the first way we can get some meaningful data and reasoning behind why past efforts failed, or didn't have the expected results.

2. How many different versions of this project have been done before

We may not be working on version 2.0 here - it could 4.0 or 6.0 - it may have a whole slew of iterations from the past which will affect what we're doing. Not only because we'll have to avoid or take into consideration the implications of those past versions of the project, but we may also have to keep in mind the side effects of the many versions of a project.

If we're working on the fourth version of a website, then we may need to be aware that the past data may not be compatible with what we plan on implementing. Having that knowledge beforehand could save us lots of time and energy.

Question #3: How can I make sure that what I create can be isolated if need be?

I'm sure you're confident that what you create won't break the internet, so to speak. That it won't cause major disruptions in what the business is doing, and there won't be any nightmare stories in *your* upcoming book.

But that's not always the case, and we want to make sure we create contingency plans for that happening. This question is integral in the cover your butt sense - making sure that what we create can be isolated or rolled back to a previous version if issues arise is a solid plan of attack for any project.

If we make a mistake, if something is unaccounted for, if another person inadvertently applies a change which causes issues - we need to be able to quickly and swiftly address the issue.

Even if it means removing our hard work, and putting in place what was there before.

It's hard to think about, but totally necessary. If I had asked myself this question before starting into that project, I would have absolutely made backups and contingency plans to ensure I could quickly roll back to a previous version of their website and buy myself time to figure out what went wrong and where.

Asking ourselves these questions, and making sure we have the entire project situation mapped out and planned for, will save us immense amounts of time, energy, and money in the long run. It's what Secret Weapons do to make sure their projects run smoothly and ensure that their clients never have to deal with a project run awry in their business.

It takes some up-front work and it takes thoughtful, considerate planning, but it's more than worth it in the long run.

TL:DR

- Making sure you assess the entire situation of a project or task before you start will save you countless hours of frustration and lost time or money.
- A hired gun will dive into a project and not worry about who or what it affects in any given business.
- A Secret Weapon will ask the right questions, and assess how the project fits into the landscape of the existing business structure to make sure it will succeed at achieving the end goals, and won't adversely affect any other part of the business.
- Ask yourself and the client these three questions before starting any part of the project work:
    1. What areas of their business does this project affect?
    2. What came before, and why did it not work?
    3. How can I make sure that what I create can be isolated if need be?

SHARING OUR KNOWLEDGE

When I was first starting out as a graphic designer in 2003 after graduating from college, I was thirsty for information. The program I completed gave us a cursory introduction to graphic design and taught us the basics, but didn't go into a huge amount of detail into advanced techniques or the various styles, techniques or methods the most successful designers were using.

So I sought it out. I felt there were missing pieces in what I knew - from how to use specific pieces of software, to ways of creating the beautiful designs I saw around me, to why the designers created their pieces like they did.

I found many amazing blogs, websites, and resources that taught so much more than what I had learned in school. I continued my education myself, through both practicing what I knew in my job, and also doing small side projects and fun pieces for freelance clients.

When I started to learn how to code and create websites, I did the same thing. I searched online and found mentors, teachers, and resources who gave freely of their time and knowledge to help others. They taught me more than I learned in college about web design, and I've continued to seek out answers and resources to solve problems, give me new ideas, and provide inspiration for what is possible in the industry.

Without these amazing people, the ones who freely gave of their time and knowledge, I wouldn't be where I am today, and I certainly wouldn't know half of what I do. They were the bridge between my formal education and the real world, and I owe them more than I can say.

When you were first starting in your business, or when you decided to pursue your career - where did you go? Did you seek out a formal education, or did you open up Google and start searching?

For the majority of us service providers, we did the latter. We found the answers we needed from various places online, and put it to use to help us grow our skills and our business. You gathered the info you needed from someone gracious enough to share their knowledge and their own processes, someone who selflessly gave it away, expecting very little, if anything, in return.

Now that I'm at the point where I can be considered an expert in what I do, I keep this in mind, and work hard to give back to the people who are in the same situation I was in 16 years ago. I firmly believe that for most service providers, you don't need a college education to be just as good as someone with a piece of paper.

Just look around you, and you'll find plenty of graphic designers who used to be philosophy grads, marketing specialists who used to be lawyers, and heck, I even know a web developer who used to be a doctor! It's these stories that inspire me to give back, and I think when we examine a bit further as to why sharing what you know is not only good for business, but good for your Secret Weapon karma points, you'll see this philosophy will do far more good for your business than anything else.

Why Don't Service Providers Share More?

The biggest pushback I've gotten from service providers on this concept of sharing what you know has been the sentiment that they will somehow cripple their business if they're giving it all away for free.

This is not only a very shortsighted view but one which leaves us in a situation bordering on paranoia. This is absolutely no way to live, so let's flip the script a bit so you can see it from another viewpoint.

Let's say you're a social media manager for your clients. You follow the best practices, and you have your own unique way of creating content for your clients that gets them great results and increases their engagement, their traffic, and their sales from their social media efforts.

If you take a look at the way you work, I imagine we could say about 15% of what you do is completely unique to yourself. The other 85% is not proprietary knowledge, and probably could be found with a bit of searching and a bit of practice.

With this in mind, the 85% of what you know and how you do things is not special and is probably the exact same techniques done by your competition. It's the 15% that makes you unique - the way you run your business, the tricks you've learned over the years to make yourself more efficient, or the techniques you've tested which have proven successful.

It can be disheartening to be told what we do is not really that special, but when we look at it this way, it means we're not running the risk of giving out our secret sauce if we share the 85% of what we do that isn't proprietary. This frees us up to share with gusto a lot of what we do! Combine that with your unique take on things, your individual way of explaining concepts, and your you-ness - you have a lot to share!

The second biggest complaint I hear from service providers is they mistakenly think if they share what they know, they'll be unwittingly training a slew of new providers who will compete with them for the same business.

It's hard thinking about how more and more people are coming online every day, and these people are hungry for a piece of the pie. They want what we have - they want a successful business, they want to provide for themselves and their family, and they want to create work they're proud of. Thinking of these people as competition is a very prevalent viewpoint, and I get how discouraging it can be to hear a client went with someone cheaper or they're complaining they can get the same services for $5 an hour from a place like Fiverr or UpWork.

Service providers who take this to heart close up and keep their information close to the chest, they don't share what they know, and this hurts their business.

Side Effects of Not Sharing May Include…

I look around at the online world today and find it much different than when I first started out. There are good things such as better platforms, amazing tools, and advances in technology that make our lives so much easier. But there's also been a shift in the air as it has become easier and easier to share.

Back in 2003, there weren't many people who were sharing what they knew freely. It was easier to find the good ones, easier to learn from them, and their message found its way into far more people's homes and businesses.

Now it's noisy.

There is a ton of information flying around, and it can be hard to sift the good from the bad, the helpful from the mundane, the gems from the rough. This can dishearten service providers. It makes us feel as though we shouldn't bother because we feel no one is paying attention. We'll be lost in the flow, a tiny voice shouting amongst millions.

This causes us to freeze, to keep our head down, to only share the great stuff and hide anything else which doesn't meet some sort of perfect standard we've set for ourselves. We don't share the in-progress stuff. We don't share the messy middle of what we're working on, so others can understand what went into making this beautiful or amazing outcome. And this leaves our sharing and content (when we do share and create content), bland and boring - it looks just like everything else, and so we do in fact slide into the background.

When we don't share what we know, there is no way for other people to know how great we are at what we do. How can someone who has a friend who needs a web designer, recommend you when they aren't aware you do web design? How can a prospect who's looking for great copywriter decide you're the one for them, when they aren't able to find any of your work or stories of the results you've created for your clients?

The main side effect of not sharing is simply stagnation - our business will not be able to grow, because no one will know about us and no one will be able to refer us as the logical choice for their projects.

The second biggest side effect is far more personal - the lack of feedback and engagement can lead to low feelings of self-worth, and make us feel as though no one cares about us or what we do.

When I'm at my lowest, in terms of how I feel about the effects and results of my work, is when I'm not sharing my process and getting feedback and engagement along the way. When I'm at my highest and feel really good about what I'm doing? That's when I'm sharing.

The reason behind this has been talked about in very bad

connotations for the last few years - and that's the dopamine hits we get when we get a thumbs up, or a like or a heart on what we share. Often talked about negatively, because the trends are overwhelmingly in favor of people relying on these hits of dopamine to signal their worth - I think in moderation, and as a method to give us motivation, they're absolutely brilliant.

We tend to work very isolated. Us and our computers, plugging away and talking to our clients, prospects, or our close friends. We close our bubbles smaller and smaller, the better we get, and the less we rely on outreach for our revenue. But the by-product of this is we don't get as much regular human interaction as we should. By sharing what we know consistently, and showing up online in various places - displaying what we're doing, sharing our thoughts on certain subjects, and showing what makes us different and special - we get some of that human interaction back, and the feedback and likes, comments and hearts, can motivate us to keep doing it.

When we close ourselves up and don't share what we know, we invite in loneliness, and I know this firsthand from my own experience. Working from home, with no one but two small boys to bounce ideas off of can be incredibly lonely. We can easily fall into the trap of thinking there's no point, because we 'only' got 10 likes on that post - when someone else got 10,000.

But the act of sharing gets us out of our comfort zone, it allows us to shake off the loneliness that comes from being an isolated service provider, and it connects us to real, live human beings - humans who absolutely can relate to what we're going, can appreciate the fine work, and offer us feedback to better ourselves.

Flipping the Script

Despite the prevalence of answers online to what can seem like every question under the sun - everything from how to debug this WordPress plugin, to how to stop our bananas from ripening so fast - I'd safely wager there is a knowledge gap out there of at least 50%.

50% of the knowledge service providers currently know is not being shared and will be lost at some point in the near future.

When was the last time you figured something out for yourself, feeling so proud and accomplished, and then had a conversation with someone more experienced and they said: "Oh yeah, I've known that for ages."

How frustrating! If they or someone like them had only shared what they knew in some form or another, you could probably have discovered it, (because I know how hard you googled to find the answer).

But by flipping that script and making sure we are the ones who are sharing what we know - we increase the chances of that knowledge never being forgotten. Or at the very least, passed on to someone else who can then share it. Like a consistent game of telephone, where the results aren't hilarious - they're timesaving and appreciated. We can be comforted by how our knowledge showcases how amazing we are at our craft, and that it also may help someone else. It might save them an hour or two of googling, or it could make the difference in them leveling up and doing better work, joining the ranks of a Secret Weapon.

Relaxing our grip on the knowledge we have, and viewing it more as a temporary loan (i.e., we get to use it now, but we have to give it back in some form or another later), shifts that mindset of everything being sacred and frees us to examine what we can share freely, without feeling as though we're giving away the golden goose to our competition.

Because when you think of it, these people are not actually your competition.

Giving away the knowledge you have may help them, yes. But it won't give them the insights you have into your process. It won't give them the experience you have. It won't help them serve their clients better like you do. It might show them an easy way to create a content calendar, but it won't show them why you came up with that calendar, and how you would adjust it for each client, based on their industry or their target market. This is all housed within that 15% special to you. The clients you want to work with, the ones best for your business - hire you for the 15%, not the 85%.

When we share what we know, and take the time to explain our process, our techniques and why we do the things we do - we move ourselves into a field where we don't have any competition. We start being viewed as the de facto expert on our topic. When clients perceive us as an expert, there's no way they'd rather go with a hired gun who's reading our articles, when they can hire the author themselves.

There is plenty of work to go around for all of us. And a true Secret Weapon knows the special way they do things, and the 15% unique to them is the reason they get hired, not because they're a graphic designer, and not because they're a copywriter - but because they were viewed as the best for the job. Because the client wanted to work specifically with you.

Ok, I'm Convinced - But Now What?

You know it's important to share, you're convinced that it will benefit yourself and others, and you're ready to get going - but now what?

If you're like me, you might get pretty overwhelmed with this at first. I've spent a lot of time trying to figure out the best way to share, what to share, and how to share it so it works out in everyone's favor. I've spent an agonizingly long time spinning my wheels, trying to figure how to do this the 'right' way, so I didn't muck it up.

But the truth of the matter is, there is no *right* way to do this, but there are guiding principles I've found that work wonders. Let's talk about those first, so you can use them to further to shape your own special way of sharing what you do, and get the highest return from your effort.

Because when it comes down to it, yes, sharing can alleviate the loneliness, sharing can foster communication, and sharing can help others find the info they need. But the bottom line here, is that sharing what we know has a purely selfish motivation behind it - to get us more business.

Consistency is Key

The first guideline I've very much learned the hard way, is that being consistent is the most important part of any sort of sharing strategy or plan. This is the one factor that will help you the most above all else. It's also the one thing I'm the worst at, (and generally the one thing service providers struggle with the most). Being consistent in when you post, and the frequency of it works in two ways - first, it gets you into the habit of sharing frequently and second, it makes sure your prospects and potential clients actually see what you're producing.

For years I followed the, 'build it and they will come' mentality. If I published a blog, I would post it randomly a few times a year, and put out social media posts whenever I 'felt like it.' I assumed people would see, and that they would flock to me. The reality is the majority of people thought, "who are you and why should I care?"

Ouch.

It was only when I decided to try my hand at a 100 days of creativity challenge that the idea of consistency really sunk home for me. Over the course of 100 days I posted one picture on instagram of my burgeoning watercolor painting. It was a fun project, it got me creating and it got to the point that posting the picture every day became a habit. Lo and behold, at the end of the challenge I was up over 600 followers. It was quite a feat for someone who, A) doesn't teach, do or offer watercolor painting as a service, and b) had never posted consistently before in her life.

That challenge taught me the power of consistency in a way no-one telling me about it would have. Seeing the real, raw proof of how the simple act of showing up each and every day in one particular space grew my audience by such a huge amount was pretty hard to ignore.

Once I stopped the challenge, I went back to my old ways of never really posting much and sure enough, my account didn't grow, no one commented, and I lost a bunch of those followers because they were expecting an image a day, and I was now producing nothing.

Being consistent can take many different forms. It doesn't have to be a post per day on our social media profiles. It can be a newsletter every two weeks to our clients. It can be a blog post each week on our website. It can be a weekly live on Facebook, where we talk about what we're working on. There are so many options and ways we can be consistent, but the underlying principle remains the same.

Once we commit to sharing something at a specific interval, it's then important to keep that up. In the beginning, don't go overboard and promise yourself you'll write a blog post a day - make it reasonable and easy to accomplish, and you can always adjust and increase it down the road.

Being consistent will build the habit of sharing so it becomes second nature - just something you do. It will also train your audience to expect to hear from you, or see something in a specific interval, and they'll start looking for your posts, your blog articles, and your live videos, because it's become as much a part of their habits as yours.

Narrowing Your Focus

Some say to share everything you know. That's great advice in general, but I take a slightly different view - share what you know, within a given topic.

It can be easy to talk about everything we do. If you're a typical service provider in the online space you probably do a bit of this, a bit of that, and some of that over there. But when you're sharing about all of those skills, projects, or talents you can easily leave people confused or unclear about what you actually do.

This is why it's important to curate what we talk about just a little bit to ensure we're focused on a specific topic or area of expertise. When we narrow it down just a bit, we're better able to communicate clearly what it is we do, within the buckets people will put us in.

When I was first starting out, I railed against this idea. I thought to myself, "but I want to do this… and I want to share that, and God forbid people not know I also do this!"

I would share everything I know about canning vegetables or crochet - but it didn't help me get clients for my business and left me with a whole lot of nothing to show for it.

No one knew what I did, and they were left with a vague impression that maybe I did websites? It obviously didn't go so well for me in terms of creating a name for myself as the Secret Weapon they would want to work with.

When I realized my posts, blog articles, and all the stuff I was sharing looked like a pretty big 'ol hot mess of nothing special, I started to look into why and found the idea of niching down. There are two ways of viewing niching down - one is you only serve a specific type of person, and the other is you only do a specific type of work.

For a web person like myself, it could mean only talking about the websites I create. Or for a Virtual Assistant, it could mean only talking about the social media management you offer. If you're a copywriting, you could focus solely on the blog articles you write. Whatever the thing is - by narrowing your focus, you're able to take advantage of people's tendency to label and classify things. You're putting yourself in a box so they don't have to do it themselves.

Does it restrict the number of topics you can freely talk about? Yes.

Does it mean you can't offer those other services, or do those other types of projects? No. Absolutely not.

Niching can be scary, and talking about one thing to the exclusion of all else can at first seem boring, or as if you're not as well rounded as you truly are. But in the end, it actually brings us more of the clients we want, because they know for sure we are the person they need for their project, because we're the one who talks about it so much.

You are not restricted to only taking projects of that sort moving forward. If someone comes to you and asks, "hey do you also do this?" if it's in your wheelhouse, then absolutely you can say yes to the project and have fun doing it. Niching down just means you are targeting you message to a specific niche, not that you're married to it for life and need to be faithful.

Go ahead and narrow down the topics you talk about. Make it clear to your audience what you do, and how you do that specific thing. There's no rule that says down the road you can't shift it and talk about other things. But, making sure you talk about one service, one type of result, and one area of expertise will help you enormously, especially in the beginning.

What Should You be Sharing?

For a service provider, there are two main categories for what we should share - what we do and why we do it.

All other types of content, categories, or message types can be easily assembled into these broader topics, and they combine to create a whole message which clearly tells our audience and prospects why we're the best fit for the job.

The first category - what we do - seems simple enough right? This is all about the work we're doing right now, the work we've done in the past, and the results we've gotten for our clients.

We can further break this down into sharing content, such as works in progress, and behind the scenes glimpses of our process for completing a project; to case studies and lessons learned from past projects. This category is firmly rooted in the actual deliverables we provide, and the quality of work we do. It's meant to showcase us in the best light possible.

The second category is all about why we do it, and has the most room for play in terms of type of content and topics we can share. Everything from our own personal motivation to what sets us apart from other providers, to industry topics, to our own take on projects and services offered by others.

This is where we get to show more of our personality, apart from the work we do, and brings more of our own voice to our industry. This category can be further broken down into more personalized sharing topics, such as a glimpse into our lives behind the work we do, the journey we took to get where we are today, and the lessons we've learned along the way. This book is a perfect example of the second category - it's all about what I've learned over the last 16 years that led me to where I am today.

The second category is where many service providers get tripped up, because it's the one with far fewer rules. It can seem as though it has the least face value in terms of showcasing how we can help others. I mean, shouldn't people who want to work with us be more interested in the work we do? But in fact, the people who want to work with us are far more interested in this category than the first. Sure, they want to know the quality of work we do and the results we bring to our clients, but knowing the motivation behind it, the real person behind the work, is far more valuable to them in terms of building up their know, like, and trust of us.

The second category showcases us as individuals, while the first category showcases our work. We need both in balance, in order to solidify our expertise in the minds of our prospective clients, and appear as a three dimensional being online.

Making it Easy

We all wish there were a magic easy button for sharing our work online. But for the most part, we tend to view sharing our work and creating content we can promote ourselves with as a much harder and bigger project than it actually is.

The key is the timeline. We're so used to thinking in a hired gun mentality where a project has a start, middle, and end. Promoting ourselves, and sharing what we know is not so cut and dry, there is no middle, and there certainly is no end. It's something we need to do every day in order to continue getting new clients and new projects.

There are two techniques I've used, which have helped me immensely in this area, and not only do they help with the whole, "what the hell do I talk about?" factor, but they also help with the consistency factor as well.

The first is a content mind map. Using this idea, we can easily create a mind map of 100+ topics we can write about easily at the drop of a hat. The concept is you would take your business or overall industry, as the central node. From there, you can identify say four to five main categories you deal with in your work. For example, if you're a copywriter you could say your four categories are writing for sales, email marketing, psychology of copywriting, and doing the writing. From your four main categories, you can then chunk it up into smaller categories and topics, until you have 10-15 topics in each of those larger four categories. Once we've done this exercise, it's easy to see we have well over 100 things to talk about.

When we keep doing this mind map technique, we can dive deeper and deeper into each topic. We can add more categories, we can add the pros and cons of each topic we came up with, we can write about these things again and again - and they're all directly related to our specific field, our specific services, and our specific way of doing things.

The second technique, which will help you immensely in sharing consistently, is a content calendar. Something you can plan out at least a week in advance what you're going to write about, how you're going to talk about it, and where you'll do this sharing.

It doesn't have to be fancy - it can be a glorified bullet list, or a full-blown digital calendar. But having these topics pre-arranged and pre-assigned for us takes away the, "what the hell do I talk about?" factor, which leaves us paralyzed each day when we fire up Facebook or Instagram or our blog.

Using both the content mind map and the content calendar will make this much easier, and I know it's helped me immensely in the long run. It stops me from going overboard, and it helps me avoid the burnout that comes from feeling as though I'm sharing too much, or that it's taking away from my client work.

Show up and Share

If there's anything I've learned, it's this: when I show up and share what I know - people respond. Sometimes it's just likes and comments, but sometimes it's referrals and new projects. There's no direct control over the outcome of sharing what you know. I wish I could sit here and tell you the exact formula I've used to get more money in my business bank account from this strategy - but I simply don't have one. When you're a service provider, the only correlation I've seen is a general upward climb - and in the long run, that's the best thing you can see in any business.

Share what you know - be seen as the expert in your field. Show off your amazing work, and post glimpses into the motivation and the person behind the work. It can only bring good things for your business, and for you personally.

Don't let the knowledge you've worked so hard for be lost, and pass it along to the next generation of Secret Weapons. Own your expertise, and make sure everyone in your network knows how much of a badass you are.

TL:DR

- Sharing what you know is not only good for business, but it's almost a moral duty to pass along the information you know to others in your field.
- When you share what you know, you set yourself up as the logical choice for new prospects, because you're displaying how much you know about your field of expertise.
- Being consistent is the most important part of sharing.
- Everyone you're sharing with is technically your audience, don't shy away from that term.
- There are two main categories of sharing - what you do, and why you do it.
- Two techniques which can help you come up with content and staying consistent are the content mind map and the content calendar.
- Sharing what you know WILL increase your visibility and make you the expert in your field, this will bring you more business, guaranteed.

A SECRET WEAPON GETS THE BEST CLIENTS

Every service provider wants to fill their client roster with the very best of clients.

We want clients who are friends, who understand what we're capable of doing, who know our boundaries and respect us enough not to cross them. We love these types of clients - we're constantly searching for more clients exactly like them.

The search for our very best clients is what defines us as a service provider. When we know exactly who we can serve best, and the types of people and companies we want to work with, we're better able to focus our efforts on finding more of them. This search inevitably shapes the services we offer, how we provide those services to our clients and the processes by which we deliver. When we get it all tuned into shape, it's like one of those perpetual motion machines we all stare so wondrously at in museums. The fewer the bumps, hiccups, and roadblocks in our path, the more enjoyable our work is, and the more time we can spend doing that work, instead of searching for more clients to fill our business machine.

Many of us can get caught up in the day to day of our to-do list. We focus on the tasks we have coming in and the output going out - it's what we love to do right? I've never been happier than when I have a large project to work on, and I can just sit down and pick up where I left off day after day, seeing progress and doing what I do best.

We get into our line of work because we love what we do. We enjoy the work, and if you don't enjoy the work, then I strongly suggest some soul searching, because there is no info in this book on finding what you love, only in finding joy in the doing of it.

But somewhere along the way of doing what we love, we get caught in a trap. I call it the more client trap.

Now, instead of doing what we love and interacting with the clients we respect and enjoy working with, we spend the majority of our time marketing our services, doing outreach, posting on social media, and answering questions to give value to others and show our expertise. It's become less about doing the work, and more about showing the persona of an expert.

I get it, really, for any business to survive and thrive we need to employ marketing and sales techniques to keep the proverbial machine running. But for the last 16 years, I've been consistently searching for ways to make it less painful. To make it just a bit more enjoyable, so the search for more clients who fit our own specific definition of 'the one' is easier and more fun.

The strategies and techniques I'm going to talk about here in the upcoming chapters are not brand new, nor are they completely unique. But I've tweaked them over the years to make them easier to execute, tailored for a service provider, and leave a much better taste in our mouth than the standard marketing tactics we've all come to know and loathe.

Marketing is a vital part of our business. We need to be able to communicate what we do and why we are the most logical choice, to the people who want to buy from us. When we boil it down to this simple statement, it certainly feels easy, even if the execution of it most certainly isn't.

Every day we're bombarded with a new way of doing marketing which promises to be better than the last, only to sadly let us down, be too complex, or too ill of a fit for our small, service-based businesses. I struggled with this for years. I chased every shiny rabbit that hopped along my path, promising to lead me to the land of higher income and exciting opportunities. Most of these bunnies ran out of breath halfway down the trail, or unraveled into a ball of string shortly thereafter, being made of no substance.

I want to help you avoid chasing those same rabbits. Because when I started focusing on the very basics, and did them consistently over and over again, that's when I truly started seeing the best results. It wasn't sexy, it wasn't an overnight success story, and it definitely wasn't something you'd see highlighted. But it worked, consistently. Sometimes when you're in business for yourself, and especially when you're the one doing the work, it's more important to focus on the consistent rather than the impressive.

We all know what happened to the tortoise and the hare, so let's stop chasing those bunnies trying to get to the end first, and instead make meaningful progress.

FOLLOWING UP

In 2015, I followed some really bad advice.

Advice so bad, it had lasting and serious effects on my business, which took months and months to recover from. It was the type of advice that seems like a really great idea at the time, but you don't really see the effects of it until you're broke and wondering why.

Let's rewind to 2015, and I'll tell you more about it - hopefully you won't make the same mistake I did, and you'll avoid any sort of debacle like this in your own business.

It was the summer of 2015, and we were just getting ready to move into our new home. The paperwork was signed, the old home had officially sold and we were now just dotting I's and crossing the T's - while also trying to pack up an entire house with two children underfoot.

I felt expansive, I felt abundant and I knew things were looking up. Our new home was gorgeous, way bigger, and the new city we were moving to was exactly what we needed as a family - small, cozy and had access to high speed internet.

Looking back, I can see exactly where I went wrong. I should have focused on the move and getting our affairs in order. I should have spent time enjoying our new situation and working towards making the whole experience as ideal as I could.

But is that what I did?

Nope.

I decided I was going to invest in a new program that was oh so shiny looking. The concept behind the program was innovative, and the end results it promised were almost too good to be true. I took the plunge and invested money I didn't really have, knowing in my heart if everything went as planned, I would make it back tenfold after applying what I learned in the program.

But I never made that money back.

The basic premise behind this program was to position yourself as an expert, which is all well and good - no complaints about that. The second premise was to base your project pricing on a percentage of the revenue the client would earn as a result of your work.

Unfortunately, the main side effect of these two concepts were you ended up making the people who wanted to work with you jump through a series of complicated hoops during the process. Once they jumped through all these hoops, the pricing for the project was often so high as to be unreasonable for any client coming in the door.

The process was convoluted. The gatekeepers and processes we had to put in place for someone to even start expressing interest in working with us was intense. It promised more interested, and committed clients, the ones who actually did all this work were the ones who would be the best to work with. But the end result was far fewer leads to begin with, and the ones who did actually make it through to the end of the intake process were the types of clients I didn't want to work with - the ones who were control freaks, who wanted everything a certain way, and were not interested in working with a Secret Weapon - they wanted a hired gun.

I followed this way of getting client leads and managing my intake process for about five months before I realized I was on the fast track to business ruin. The daunting process turned away about 90% of people who expressed interest in working with me. Of the 10% who made it through, they were either not a good fit personality-wise, or they had far more time than money on their hands, so their budgets were small, and the projects were more hassle than they were worth. It was disastrous for my business. If it weren't for a few solid, long term clients, I would have been out of business and looking for an office job.

But the biggest downfall of this new way of running our lead generation and project pricing structure was that it told us we didn't need to follow up - it put the ball in the client's court at all times and depended on them to expend the effort to work with us.

It was disastrous.

After realizing just how much of a negative effect this way of thinking and doing was having on my business, I decided to closely examine what I had changed in order to follow this 'new way' and discover the biggest culprit costing me clients and projects.

I found two significant leaks - the first being how hard it was for people to actually get information about working with us. In order to find out any information, prospects had to fill in a three-part form with over 20 questions. It wasn't an easy process at all, and while being effective at turning away the tire kickers, it also cost us the opportunity to use our sales muscles to turn maybes or tire kickers into yeses.

The second major issue I saw with this new system was it didn't advise us to follow up with the people who had received proposals. It had us sit back and wait for them, because that meant they were 'serious' about working with us.

But what if someone was serious and they just got caught up in the day to day working of their business (like, ahem, everyone does), and what if they just needed a gentle reminder about where we left off, and the opportunity to rekindle a conversation?

This severe lack of direction when it came to follow-ups set my business back at least a year by the time I recovered. And the first thing I did? I followed up with each and every person I had contact with during the time I was following the program, and within three weeks had four new projects.

The Rise of the Ghost

We laugh about how people are ghosting each other in the online dating world, but this phenomenon has been present in the business community for ages. As professionals and as business owners, we've probably had our fair share of ghosting experiences - either as the ghost or by a ghost.

From clients who disappear after we send them a proposal or a contract, to contractors or outsourced workers who never respond to our feedback, to the people in our professional communities who just one day go poof! Ghosting has many different forms, and it's everywhere.

Professional ghosting costs Secret Weapons thousands of dollars a year in unearned work and ruined reputations. While we can gnash our teeth and shake our fists in the air at the client who ghosted us, and the lost projects as a result, it turns out that the simplest of strategies is the solution, and it's one we need to be consistently using in our business for growth - the art of the follow up.

I Ain't Afraid of No Ghost

While we can discuss what's causing this ghosting behavior, and why it's become so prevalent in the modern gig economy, I think the most important thing we can focus on is our own activities when it comes to avoiding being ghosted.

When I realized I was losing clients left, right, and center in my business, and no new clients were coming in; I hit the proverbial pavement. I emailed, called, texted, and sent smoke signals to every single prospective client I had within the last six months.

During that time, I asked some very embarrassing questions and set myself up for some very negative feedback. And while it was a bit of an ego blow to get the feedback all at once, I could have received it piecemeal if I had just followed up periodically over time.

The most significant piece of feedback I received from all those clients was that it was too hard to work with me. They felt as though I wasn't involved enough in the process, and wasn't interested in working with them - they didn't feel as though I was passionate about the projects they wanted to create.

This was a big by-product of the hands-off approach the program I had been following was teaching. It went on and on about how to position yourself as an expert, but it kept you aloof and put far too many gatekeepers between you and your clients.

After I licked my wounds and realized exactly where the holes were in this process, I weighed its merits and its down points, and created a franken-followup monster which has served me wonderfully since then.

By using this follow up system methodically each and every week, I'm able to stay top of mind with my clients and prospects, and we get to an eventual yes or no much faster than if I had waited for them to take the initiative to make a decision.

At first I thought I was pestering them - would they feel like I was bothering them if I emailed them several times over the course of two weeks? Would they think less of me? That I was desperate for the work? How would I maintain the expert status I wanted to preserve, while still using the power of following up?

The Franken-FollowUp Monster System

I arrived at this system completely by accident. It came about when something went horribly wrong in an automation I had created to follow up with clients after I sent an invoice or proposal. The basic premise was this: if after seven days after sending the invoice or the proposal, the invoice hadn't been marked paid or the proposal marked as accepted, it would send out a lovely email asking if the client had any questions, or if they would like to click here to accept and/or pay.

It was super simple - one message, one email, nothing too overly complex.

But it turned into an autoresponder monster after I hit play on the feature. Unbeknownst to me, I had set it up wrong. Being a pretty new piece of software, and me just wanting to get up and running with it, I entered the wrong number into some fields, and the autoresponder ended up sending them a message every single day for seven days afterwards, instead of my desired one email after seven days.

I started to get a few... odd client comments and responses after about a week.

"I know this is really important to you, so I'll be sure to get you that info in the next day or so."

"I love your initiative, but we're going to put this on hold for a few weeks until we sort out the budget."

"YES! Okay, let's go ahead with this."

"Wow, you are persistent! Okay, let's talk about how we can adjust the proposal to include my new Youtube channel graphics as well."

After this went on for about a week, one client straight up called me and said, "Gabby, we want to work with you, but can you please stop emailing us every day? We're just waiting for board approval right now."

Wait, what?

Stop emailing them? I was so confused. As far as I knew, I hadn't emailed them once since I had sent off the proposal, thinking my newly created follow-up message would go out after seven days and would take care of some follow-up.

So I looked into it, and low and behold, that automation had sent out 52 emails in the last nine days to my clients.

52!

I was so embarrassed, and quickly sent a message to my clients apologizing for pestering them so much, and explaining how my software had a little glitch but that it was fixed now, and please accept my apologies and don't hate me. I received a few, "oh no worries" kind of messages in response, and I left it at that.

But then I got an email from one of my clients who runs an international sales training company. He trains top performing sales executives across the globe, and has tripled his business over the last four years since he started doing online training, (so naturally he had some input about the whole thing).

"Gabby, don't you ever apologize for following up to a customer. You pester them silly until you get a clear yes or a clear no. Only when you get one or the other, do you move onto something else."

Part of me cringed at this.

It brought up images of Glengarry Glen Ross and the slimy salesperson. Of always being closing, and of pestering people until I lose any sort of goodwill, and my own soul in the process. It felt icky, until I decided I had to look at it a different way.

I went back to the numbers and realized in those nine days where I had let loose my franken-followup monster, I had actually collected invoices faster (three days rather than the more common 12 days), and my proposals were accepted or rejected sooner (five days as opposed to the more common 21 days).

So if my invoices were paid faster, and I got a clear yes or no on a project right away, rather than wallowing in "do they love me?" purgatory for three weeks - there was certainly something to this whole follow up idea.

Obviously I didn't want to send an email a day until perpetuity, as that's just not me and not my style, (Blake from Glengarry I'm not), but I knew that obviously following up more frequently was going to bring me some positive returns in either reducing time to getting paid, freeing up brain power from fretting over invoices and proposals, and even focusing on getting more business.

It's Alive!

There are three main stages within every service provider project lifecycle. Over the years of both working in my own business, and talking with other service providers, I've realized that even though the work we do differs, these stages remain the same. The question then, is how can we optimize each stage with follow ups that allow you to stay top of mind with your clients throughout the entire lifecycle of a project?

When I first identified these stages, I realized there were a few places that a bit of up-front effort would make for big returns. And there were stages in the project where effort would instead be gradual and manual as it progresses.

Let's examine some of the followup systems I put into place in my business, and how you can set them up in yours, so you can get the benefits of following up like a Secret Weapon.

Stage 1 Follow Ups - Commit or Get Off The Field

The first stage of any project is always the most exciting - it's the one that opens up new opportunities, new clients, new income, and of course, new problems.

As a service provider, we spend the majority of our time doing the work we're hired to do. Often this can lead to gaps and procrastination on the things we know we should be doing, (like marketing and following up). Tasks we know have the biggest impact on our business overall.

It's damn hard to do things like sending a follow up email when we're looking at our to-do list that's a mile long for the day. Those tasks get pushed to the bottom or moved to tomorrow - over and over again.

The first stage of the project flow is pretty simple in theory. A person reaches out with an idea or a project they want to get more info and pricing on, we follow up and have some back and forth before we deliver a proposal or quote to them. They review said quote, and either accept, or ask for any revisions or scope changes.

Stage 1 is where the majority of service providers have the most leaks, where the system I tried to follow before this point, failed. If we think about it - this first stage is the most vital part of any business. This is the stage where we win or lose the client.

It stands to reason the first stage is where we'll get the most return for optimizing our follow ups. This is where the power of following up with consistency will make the most difference. Creating a series of follow ups that aligned with the tasks and milestones of this stage can bring great returns.

I created a series of emails that would align with when a prospect first reached out, with the goal of getting them to fill in a form or booking a call with me so I could get the information about their project and the information I need to give them an accurate price.

I started asking myself a whole bunch of What Ifs - what if they don't fill in the form or book a call after X number of days? What if they fill in the form, but I need more info from them? What if I'm not able to help them based on their business or their project?

Using these what ifs to guide me, I mapped out several different situations, and the follow up emails which would align with both their actions and inactions.

When you first plan this out it may seem a bit convoluted, but if you start following the paths of what ifs you'll see it makes logical sense, and a typical client certainly wouldn't be bombarded with emails or feel as though they were being aggressively sold to at this point (less Blake from GlenGarry and more Ross from Friends at this point).

The whole point of the Stage 1 follow ups should be to gather the information we need and to get the client to make a decision one way or another to work with us. We want to spend the least amount of our time helping our clients get to a decision. Now, don't get the impression we're not being supportive and helpful along the way. But we've got a goal here baby, and these follow ups are going to help us accomplish that.

Stage 2 Follow ups - Info Gathering and Legal Stage

Once we have a decision one way or another from our prospective client, it's time to move onto Stage 2 in the follow up system we created. If our client decided not to work with us on this project, then Stage 2 is pretty straightforward, and simply asks them for more feedback on the process of going thought Stage 1 with us.

There is only 1 email in Stage 2 if the client has decided not to go ahead. It asks for feedback on the process, ways we can make the process better, and getting more information on why they decided to not proceed or work with us specifically.

I urge you to not skip this valuable email. It's easy to think, "well, that's that and there's no sense in wasting any more time or energy on this prospect." But I find the best feedback I get is from prospects who decided not to work with me. That's where I discovered the holes in my franken-follow up sequence to begin with, and that's where I get the most valuable feedback in terms of how I can tweak the process, wording changes which may have made the project go a different way, or even if my pricing is below or above what they were expecting.

This email gives us some incredibly juicy details to work with, and offers insight into why things are going smoothly or where we can improve our process of working with prospects.

If our client does agree to go ahead with working with us, they love the proposal, and they're chomping at the bit to get started, then we proceed to the second branch of the Stage 2 follow ups.

This is the information gathering and legal stage of things. It is at this point that we're making sure we get everything we need to deliver an amazing project to our client, and ensure we didn't miss anything in the scope or delivery. This helps us create an accurate project profile to use moving forward.

At this point, since I'm using an automated system to deliver my follow up sequence, it automatically puts them into my onboarding sequence where I send them a contract, the first invoice, and introduces them to the client portal I use to manage my projects.

If the client fills everything out in a timely manner, then the steps go by pretty sequentially, but since we're focusing on following up and we don't want to chase our clients manually for this information, there are several email prompts built-in to make sure the info is submitted in a timely manner, so the project deadlines are honored, and there's no lollygagging through this important part of a new project.

When I'm confident I have everything I need, the onboarding sequence gets marked as complete, and we move the project into Stage 3 of the followup sequence. This stage is designed to make sure our clients fall in love with our processes, and keep coming back for more.

Stage 3 Follow ups - The Magic

I call Stage 3 the magic stage because this is where many follow up sequences stop, and the hired gun falls behind the Secret Weapons of the world.

When we first start a project is when a client is at their most vulnerable. Every single one of our clients is second guessing themselves at this point - did they make the right decision? Was their investment worth it? Are we going to deliver what was promised? Will they like it? Is it going to be as successful as they hope and dream?

All very valid feelings and emotions from their end of the project. If you're a true Secret Weapon, and you charge premium rates for your very valuable services - then the Stage 3 follow ups are proof you're worth that high investment.

Many service providers get caught in the two mode trap - one mode is doing the work. Head down, focused on the to-do list, and the projects before them. The other mode is client mode - getting and communicating with clients, trying to woo them to work with us, and keep them happy after they do. Switching back and forth can be painful, because it uses two very different parts of our brain.

The first part - project mode, is where we're the most comfortable. It requires the creative parts of our brain, and it's where we excel. Doing the work, honing our craft, and being productive. Publishing, creating, and doing what we love.

The second mode is harder, it requires the logical, and most importantly, unemotional side of our brains. It means we have to follow set systems, set aside our feelings and hopes, and perform more traditional sales-oriented tasks.

Stage 3 is all about bringing us out of that creative mode, and putting us into the logical side more often, so we get used to doing it on a consistent basis. We do this by creating a set follow up schedule for each project, and creating reporting that's baked into our projects.

By reporting on our progress - what we've done, what we're going to do, and any issues that have come up - as we're going through the project, we experience two major side effects. The first side effect is we put the client at ease, and they feel like they're being kept in the loop on what's going on with their project. The second side effect is any issues which arise can be dealt with swiftly, so we can easily get back to the head down working mode without any roadblocks or bottlenecks.

What I've done in my business, is to create what I call the weekly check-ins. This is a simple email template I've saved in my Gmail that I recycle for each client, and send on a weekly basis. For me it's Fridays, because I like the sense of wrapping things up for the week, and it helps both me and my clients stay on track on a weekly schedule for the project.

In this email template I have:

1. A 2-3 sentence blurb on what was accomplished that week.
2. A 2-3 sentence blurb explaining what I plan on doing the next week.
3. A 2-3 sentence blurb on anything I'll need from the client to accomplish the tasks the next week, or any issues I've come across that need any action or input from them.
4. A general update on how I believe the project is going so far, and any adjustments to timelines I believe will need to be made (whether getting done faster or slower than originally proposed in the scope of the project).

That's it - just four things, and for each client I estimate it takes me approximately 4 minutes to write up one of these update emails.

The difference I've seen in my projects has been astounding since I've started implementing these Stage 3 update emails. Not only have I gotten great feedback from my clients about how they love them and feel as though they constantly know what's going on in their projects, but it also has an added side effect of planning my next week for me.

By taking those blurbs about what I plan to do the next week, I can more effectively gauge my workload and lighten the Monday morning stupor, which can come from not having a plan of action. I essentially create my next week's to-do list on Friday of the week before. It lets me relax and enjoy my weekend with my family, not worrying about what I might have to do on Monday.

Following Up Works

It's a simple concept right? But the simplest of concepts are the ones hardest to implement, because they're so deceptive in their simplicity. We look at them and think, "This can't possible work, it's too easy," and so we look for a more complex solution to our issue.

I stumbled upon the importance of following up quite by accident - first by seeing the effects of not following up (and ouch did those effects hit my bottom line), and then seeing the effects of following up too much (definitely wore out my welcome with a few clients). Finding the happy middle where I wasn't a ghost, but I also wasn't hammering on people's digital doors every day made the most amount of sense.

When you break down the follow up process into these three stages, you'll see it becomes much easier to implement within your own business. It's going to be easy to set up, easy to track, and easy to see where you can make improvements to get better results.

Not seeing much of a difference in your Stage 1? Perhaps adding a few more nudge emails can help your clients make a decision faster, so you can either secure them as a client or move on to other things. Remember, you're not being pushy or inconsiderate here - in fact you're being inconsiderate to both their time and yours by leaving open loops where no one has made a clear decision one way or another.

If you find your clients are 'checking in' too often for your liking, when you're in the process of fulfilling your project duties, then perhaps you need to beef up your Stage 3 follow ups, so you can keep them in the loop, unclog the bottlenecks, and sway their insecurities about working with you on their projects.

All of these follow up strategies are going to help position you as the logical choice to work with in the future. When your clients are happy and well taken care of, they'll come back again and again, because they enjoy the experience of working with you so much.

TL:DR

- Following up is one of the things that sets a Secret Weapon apart from a hired gun. A hired gun goes in, does the work, and gets out. A Secret Weapon establishes trust and respects their time and the time of the client too much to let things go unsaid and decisions go unmade.
- By breaking your follow up sequence into three distinct stages, you can create a strong follow up system that moves your clients from initial contact into completed project faster and more efficiently, with less management on your part.
- Stage 1 of your follow ups is designed to get them from prospect to either a paying client, or moving to another solution as fast as possible.
- Stage 2 of your follow ups is designed to make sure you get all the I's dotted and the T's crossed, so you can get started on the project with everything you need.
- Stage 3 is about supporting your client as you go through the project, and making sure they stay in the loop on what's going on at all times.
- Put them all together and what have you got? A Secret Weapon follow up sequence that gets you and your business big results.

BUILDING A REFERRAL ENGINE

What is it about the service providers who have people constantly talking about them, telling others, and growing their business with seemingly no effort on their part?

It's not voodoo witchcraft, and it certainly isn't that they're magnitudes better than you - it's something so simple, many service providers look over how powerful it can be to grow and expand their business.

It's referrals.

Service providers who have a good referral system get clients again and again without having to put up neon signs, use advertising, and spend all day on advertising. They focus on doing great work, and having other people spread the word for them. Referrals aren't just a nod in your direction. They have the power to completely transform the trajectory of your profits, your satisfaction, and your ability to get and keep the ideal clients you're looking for.

Becoming the person everyone refers others to isn't some sort of magic sweet spot you'll achieve one day if you put in the effort and the sweat hours. It's something the best service providers make a priority in their business day in and day out.

Being referable is only half the equation. Yes, we need to be good at what we do. Yes, we need to serve our clients, so they're tickled pink from working with us, and yes, we absolutely need to get them the results from the projects we complete for them. When we become a Secret Weapon, we make the task of referring us incredibly easy because we are indeed, referable.

But the other half of the equation comes from encouraging, promoting, and strongly suggesting that the wonderful clients you're working with do their best to refer you to their likewise wonderful colleagues, friends, neighbors, and anyone else they come across.

We're going to go into more detail on how we can create a referral engine that brings us constant sources of pre-warmed prospects who are already aware of exactly how great we are - no convincing required.

There are plenty of service providers who have built successful and profitable businesses based solely on referrals - I know because I'm one of them.

From 2003 to about 2017, I didn't do one lick of advertising or promoting myself, other than a few spots here or there in my clients work. I never put a link back to my website in the footer of the projects I built. There was never a "Made by 12Strong" mark anywhere on what I created for my clients.

I rarely talked about what I did on social media, and other than the blog posts on my website I published sporadically, there was very little in the way of marketing I was doing for my own business.

And yet I grew. I got new clients each and every month, as the number of people who referred me grew and grew over the years.

The reason this worked so well was because I made asking for, rewarding, and promoting referrals my top strategy for acquiring new business. It was the backbone of the company I built. It served me well while my little ones were small, and I didn't have the budget for formal advertising, or the capacity to take on large amounts of clients or huge projects.

It wasn't perfect, it wasn't 100% predictable, and it certainly isn't something I would recommend as being the only marketing tactic in our tool belt. But having a referral engine in our business is a powerful method of bringing in repeat and new business without spending a dime or countless hours online promoting ourselves. It can become a key driver of growth in our Secret Weapon business moving forward, and I encourage you to follow through on the information in this chapter as soon as you can.

Referrals by Accident or Chance

When most service providers get to a certain point in their careers, they almost always have referrals coming to them. It's the nature of being good at what we do, and the indicators that present themselves from longevity and a large body of work. But it's usually completely by accident.

It's taking advantage of human nature to share and promote something that has made their lives better. When we find a product, technique, or tool that works wonders for us - how much more inclined are we to share it with someone who has the same problem?

It's the same with referrals and the average service provider. We are rewarded by our client's natural inclination to share good things with others. The downfall of this is it is indeed, by accident - we don't take advantage of these referrals, or ask for them specifically - we sit around waiting patiently for someone, somewhere, to talk about us, and refer us to someone they know. It's passive and unpredictable.

Without a system of some sorts to make sure we make the most of these referrals to encourage or reward them, we're left to the mercy of your average referral-based business, never really knowing when the next client is coming in, and feeling stuck in our slower than molasses growth.

When we don't have these pieces of a referral system in place, it's easy to think referrals don't work and start believing avenues such as paid advertising or time-consuming social media campaigns are the only things that will. Which couldn't be further from the truth.

There's far too much left to chance when we don't have any sort of formal referral system in place. Relying on people's memories, and the stars to line up to get a referral is the standard operating procedure. Before I had my formal system in place, that was certainly me - waiting and hoping one of my clients would throw me a bone, and refer one of their colleagues to me for a new project.

But when we're stuck in that zone of waiting and hoping, we're putting the growth of our business, and the revenue coming in to complete chance.

Think about it like this; you'll have to wait for a myriad of circumstances to line up in order for your client to refer you to someone they know. The client will need to be talking to someone who is either in the same situation as them or is currently talking about a problem they think you could solve. And then once they recognize this person is in the same situation, they need to remember to refer you, and pass along your information. Plus, once the referral is made, that new person then needs to act on the referral, and either pick up the phone or fire up their email.

There are far too many moving pieces in this equation, and if any one of them isn't present, the whole thing falls apart.

We need to remove these pieces of chance from our referral engine, so not only do these referrals happen consistently, but they have fewer moving parts, and are less likely to rely completely on chance.

When we remove these elements of accident and chance from the referrals coming to us, we also get a better idea of who our most vocal and loyal clients are.

Do you know where your clients are coming from? If it's through referrals, do you know who referred them? Having some sort of referral engine in place ensures you not only can see who is referring the most people to you, but it also lets you act on that information so you can keep those referrals coming. When you have advocates of your services and business, who are willing to tell everyone they know about you - why aren't you making sure it's worth their while to keep recommending you?

For years I had no idea who was referring me to new clients - there was a period of about a year where I had six new clients come in who flat out told me they were pointed in my direction and informed I was the best. After a while, I started doing some investigating and discovered all six of these clients came from one referral source. As soon as I found out who it was I sent her a big 'ol bunch of flowers to thank her.

But if I hadn't done some digging, and if I hadn't asked who referred them, then I wouldn't have known one of my clients literally sent me over $40,000 of work in one year alone and I would have just let it slide, never making her feel appreciated for the act of spreading the word about me.

Having these systems in place do far more good than you can ever realize and if you plan on staying small in your business, there is certainly a way you can remain happily spoiled and relying entirely on a steady stream of referral business coming in through your doors.

But you need to have the engine in place so you can make sure this referral train keeps going, so let's examine the key pieces of a referral engine and how you can set the wheels in motion to bring you a constant stream of new business.

Creating Your Referral Engine

I'm going to try to keep the train references to a minimum here in this section, but I have to paint the picture for you of the power of a referral engine and how it can move your business year after year. When I speak about a referral engine, it is, in fact, useful to look at it like an engine. The train is, of course, you and your business, merrily chugging along through the mountain passes, enjoying the beautiful scenery and stopping along the way to visit gorgeous sights (oooh waterfall).

The engine making your train run is the revenue you generate to keep your train on the tracks and building forward momentum. Now we're in 1934 here in analogy land, so your train runs on a fossil fuel of some sort, something that needs to be continuously fed into the fire to keep that engine moving forward. The projects coming into your business are that power source. You need a constant stream of them to maintain the forward momentum of your train.

Here's where the referral part comes in. The referrals you get are the steady shovel, lift, toss of the engineer throwing fuel into the fire. When he gets going into a comfortable rhythm - shovel, lift, toss, shovel, lift, toss, shovel, lift, toss - he can get the engine purring like a kitten with a constant source of fuel.

When the stack of fuel runs out, or when he's off his groove and has to scramble, this slows the train down and can even stop it completely.

Our aim then is to keep the engineer in his consistent shovel, lift, toss motion over and over again so our train can keep chugging along merrily. The best way to do this is to create a formal referral program you can easily reuse for each client, so you can keep the consistent shovel, lift, toss of fuel to your train.

A formal referral program allows us to consistently bring in referrals, so we're less susceptible to the feast and famine periods of project work. It helps us grow our business in a more profitable manner by not having to use things like advertising or paid marketing channels.

When I first sat down and created my formal referral program and put it into place, I saw a big jump in the number of people who were referred to me by my existing clients. I was able to bring on at least one new client each and every month after I implemented this. It had such a huge effect on my revenue that I never looked back. Asking for the referral, rewarding my clients for referring me to people, and maintaining this program has been the cornerstone of my business ever since. Even if you're just starting out, I'm sure you'll start seeing some significant gains from it pretty quickly too.

Planning Your Referral Program

Ideally, your referral program is going to consist of three main parts - how you ask for referrals, how you track those referrals, and what you do after the referral turns into paying client.

The first part of your referral program is all about how you're going to promote it and let your clients know you encourage and reward them for referring you to their colleagues. It needs to become a cornerstone of your client onboarding and off-boarding process and mentioned throughout the process of working with you.

When bringing on a new client, we need to mention our referral program and ask them specifically to either pass along the contact info of anyone they think would be a good match for our services. At several points throughout the project, we also need to ask them again if they feel there is anyone they think would be a good fit for us and our services.

Once the project is complete, we can ask again, and a few weeks later when we check in on them, we ask again.

You might be thinking this seems like a lot of asking, doesn't it?

It is.

And it's necessary. The key behind a referral program is we're consistently asking for referrals, and by continually asking, we'll receive them. For the most part, clients do not mind you asking consistently if anyone comes to mind - in fact, it starts them thinking of who they could possibly pass along to you as potential clients. It makes it stick in their mind, which is exactly what we need for our referral program.

Getting over the feeling that we're asking for referrals is somehow us being a bother is the biggest step to creating a referral program to consistently bring in new clients. When our clients refer people to us, they get the benefit of feeling as though they are connecting people - and how do you feel when you connect people together? Probably pretty good right? I know I get a great sense of joy from seeing two people I connect go on to create great things.

Secret Weapons are dubbed so by their clients, and when we have raving fans, we need to put a bullhorn in front of their mouth so everyone can hear them. Giving our clients this opportunity is a good thing, and once we make this simple mindset shift of viewing our asking for referrals as a benefit to both parties involved, the feeling of bothering your clients goes away pretty fast.

Besides asking for these referrals frequently, we need to also mention this referral program at every opportunity we have both before, during, and after a project. This can be done by mentioning it in our email signatures, when we reach out to new prospects and when we post on social media. Reinforcing the message everywhere we can not only helps to get the word out, but it also strengthens our asking muscles, so it becomes a habit and eventually, a skill we can count on to grow our business.

Incentives for Referrals

The second part of a referral program is to offer an incentive of some sort for people to refer us. As much as we want to believe people will simply refer us based on the goodness of their heart and their high opinions of us, we know some sort of incentive will make the action a no brainer on their part. By creating an incentive, we'll help to make it more of a win-win situation for all involved and increase the chance that our clients will refer us to others more frequently.

These incentives can take many forms, but I've found the best are directly related to what we do. In my referral program, I give clients 15% off their next project if one of their referrals becomes a paying client. This encourages repeat customers and is something easy for me to do. It doesn't take money out of my pocket and has often helped me secure even larger projects down the road, since the discount entices them to go bigger.

Consider offering tiers in your referral program as well. While I offer the standard 15% for any one referral from my clients, when a client reaches five referrals, I up that to 25% to further reward them, and make it more valuable to them to keep referring people to me. Once a client reaches ten referrals, I offer them free maintenance on their website for life. Again, something easy for me to offer, and a very enticing incentive for someone who has a new site and is facing maintaining it now for the rest of its lifetime.

Incentives should be easy for us to offer and make sense in the grand scheme of what we do. I've heard of admin assistants offering referrals incentives of a free month of bookkeeping, or a custom calendar containing their client's contact's birthdays.

The best incentive I've heard is from a wood worker who has a stall at my local farmer's market - if you refer to him five new paying clients, he makes you a custom set of personalized BBQ tools. Again, something easy for him to create, and every time you use those tools for flipping burgers at your backyard parties how easy is it to tell everyone about him and what fantastic work he does?

But beware of offering misaligned incentives to your clients.

We've all heard the term freebie seekers, and I find this is so much more prevalent when the reward for taking some sort of action is not aligned with the intent or original service. Think twice before offering things like tablets, electronics, or vanity items which don't make sense when compared to what you offer as a service. These are easily forgotten, and less enticing than something more personal or customized.

Tracking Referrals

The third part of a referral program is being able to track where these new clients are coming from. Getting referrals is great, but if we don't know where they're coming from or who is referring them, then the other two parts of the program just won't work as they should. How can we reward clients for referrals, if we aren't sure if they're actually referring people to us?

This doesn't have to be incredibly complex - it can be simply ensuring every new prospect who comes to you gets asked if someone referred them and who. Making sure we can attribute the referral to a specific client is important, not only in tracking our sales numbers, but also in providing the incentives to clients who are doing the referring.

When we get bigger, we can think about using a system to automate this better, by say, giving each client a unique link they can use to refer people to, and tracking through there. But as with all technology, it isn't as foolproof as we'd like it to be, so the good old-fashioned ask is still our best method of tracking.

Making sure we're keeping track of these numbers somewhere consistent lets us tally up any client's referrals, and make sure we're staying on top of rewarding them when they refer and hit certain milestones in our referral program. I mentioned I have three distinct tiers in my referral program, so keeping track of where they are within these tiers, and how I need to reward them when they reach the next one is important to keeping the referrals pouring into my business at a consistent rate.

Start Now

Having a referral program created is one thing. Knowing what you'll offer to clients and how you'll track them is an essential first step. But the continual asking for referrals is the hard part of this process, and having the best setup and intentions can only go so far.

Start asking for referrals right now. A new referral program is something big, and definitely fodder for a client-wide email blast informing them of the new program and how it works. If you're more personalized in your approach, put it in your email signature and send out individual notes to each one of your clients informing them of the new program and explaining what's in it for them.

You're going to start seeing great results with this approach, and I promise having a referral-based business is entirely possible in this online world we live in - in fact, it's even easier now, because a referral is only an email away. Take advantage of this and have a program making it easy for people to promote their own Secret Weapon to others who can benefit from working with you.

TL:DR

- The best Secret Weapons are seemingly constantly getting referrals from their current and past clients
- It is entirely possible to have a business based completely on referrals, I did it for years, and you can to.
- Your business is a train. The projects coming in are the fuel for the engine, and the referrals you get are the shovel, lift, toss motion of the engineer throwing that fuel into the furnace, having a good rhythm is the key.
- Creating a formal referral program is the key to building up your referrals, so they're more consistent.
- Asking for referrals as many times as needed is a simple mindset shift, you're helping your clients feel good by doing the referring, not bothering them with your asking.
- A formal referral program needs three things:
    - Consistent asking
    - Incentives
    - Tracking system
- Your incentives should make sense in the grand scheme of your services and having multiple tiers of rewards increases the numbers you get.
- Ensure you have a way to track the referrals coming in, so you can offer your rewards to the clients doing the referring.
- Start today - create your referral program and begin by reaching out to your existing clients to let them know about it, start reaping the rewards of your client's good will as soon as possible.

AVOIDING THE MORE CLIENT TRAP

"How do I get more clients?"

This is the single most pervasive question service providers have.

It keeps us awake at night, it invades our thoughts when we're trying to be present with our families, and it nags at us as we try to fall asleep at night. This single thought is the driver behind the majority of our actions outside our client work and tasks.

The need for more clients is almost like a disease. It's catching.

Getting more clients is the backbone of millions of online articles and blog posts floating around the interwebs. They tell you the only key to success as a service provider is to get more clients.

And where does this leave us? Thinking the only solution to our problems is more. That if we're not getting more clients each and every day, each and every week, we're not good enough, we're not doing this whole business thing right.

They give us techniques and tools to get more clients. Techniques which make us feel uncomfortable in order to 'get our name out' or 'land clients' as though they were some hereto undiscovered tropical island we'll plant a flag on.

I call this the more clients trap - and it's got us firmly in a vise-like grip. It leaves us feeling as though we're not good enough, that we're failing as service providers and business owners because no matter how many useful tips these articles give us, they fail to identify how much is good enough. More is just a concept; it's an empty pit of expectations. Hopes and dreams wrapped in a sinking, sliding feeling of not enough.

But what if getting more clients wasn't the answer?

When I first made my foray into freelance services, I fell into this trap, hard.

I hunted down clients as though they were prey, and it made me feel as though I was willing to do anything if someone would just please hire me. The constant search for more clients was exhausting, it left me burnt out, and honestly, the clients I did get were the ones who could smell my desperation on the wind, and knew I was willing to do anything to get their business.

For the first five or six years of my business, I vacillated between needing to get more clients and becoming overwhelmed with what I "had" to do to get them. Write blog posts, network, post on social media, create an email newsletter, sending out promotional mailings, cold call businesses, get referrals, put out job for hire advertisements, and advertise in local newspapers. The list went on and on and every article I read, a different technique was introduced, which promised to be the one to get me more.

No wonder that in 2014, I almost shut down my business and got a job. The constant search for new clients was absolutely exhausting. It left me no time to actually do the work I did secure, and the rest of my life suffered terribly for it.

It was only when I decided I would focus entirely on being a referral-based business that the pressure eased up enough that I had the space to recognize the vapid, soul-sucking succubus that's been spawned in the name of more clients.

This focus on more and more clients has spawned an entire industry of marketers, business coaches, and consultants who primarily focus on getting you more clients. They might dress it up as client acquisition, audience growth, or revenue growth, but boiled down it all comes to one thing - you need more, and I'm going to help you get it.

You can't go two paces online without running into one of them, and the messages they spew about how you're somehow not good enough if you're not fully booked out, leaves us wondering if there's something wrong with us. If we're not wildly successful and have a client roster a mile long, then are we even successful? If we aren't generating scores of revenue and relaxing on a beach somewhere, (while God knows who is actually serving these clients we've acquired), then we can't consider ourselves a success.

Success Does Not Equal More Clients

What if there's nothing wrong with us for not wanting to serve hundreds of people a year? What if instead of serving as many people as we possibly can we instead focus on the chosen few who make the most difference?

What if we're not supposed to operate from a place of lack and constantly needing more and if we do, it draws from us instead of serving us?

As service providers, we are doing the work day in and day out and we like it that way. Having too many clients leaves us scattered and unable to live up to our full potential. Focused work is where we thrive, and we can't do that when we've got a plate overloaded with both project work and client attraction activities.

The constant hop from project to project can leave us on the verge of burnout, and we end each day feeling exhausted to the point of not wanting to get up the next morning. For seven years, I worked in this manner and never even questioned it - it was just what you had to do to be a successful web developer in this market.

I kept telling myself the hustle and grind were the industry and what I had gotten into. Dealing with numerous clients, the constant feeling of being interrupted, and pulled from one client to the next on a constant rollercoaster of work was just normal.

But this wasn't sustainable. For me, or for any service provider out there. We can't go on like this and expect to experience any sort of meaningful growth, both in our business and in our personal lives.

The rates of burnout are increasing more and more every year amongst the service provider industries - I see it constantly, and the fact it's being talked about more online shows the problem is only getting worse, not better.

When I was talking to Vicky, a graphic designer out of New York City, she told me how she joined a mastermind, where the leader was constantly pushing the members to get more clients. There were stats boards and races to the top, and everyone enjoyed the games at first, but she said after a while everyone started to show signs of wear and tear.

"Every week we'd show up, and the bags under our eyes were

getting deeper, we were more listless, and less engaging. It felt like the energy was being slowly sucked out of everyone in the group and when we started, we were so vibrant and excited to grow our businesses. I think about half of us ended up quitting after six months, because we just couldn't take it anymore."

Vicky ended up closing up her business, and getting a job working for an agency to recuperate from the experience. And these types of stories are everywhere. Droves of service providers, feeling as though it's their fault or there was something inherently wrong with them for not making it work.

I've personally felt the effects of burnout many times and tracing it back to the idea I needed more and more clients is easy in hindsight, but while I was in the thick of it, I couldn't understand what was wrong with me.

In 2015, I was serving about 12 clients at once, and at first I thought it was absolutely fantastic! There was a good amount of revenue coming in, and the projects I was working on were interesting and fun. But I slowly sank into a deep feeling of never being able to catch up. There were days when dragging myself out of bed to face the stream of emails, the work piling up on my plate, and the day to day struggles of running my own business was just too much.

It became a chore to get myself out of bed. I winced every time I opened my email, and the projects I was working on felt like a three-hundred-pound weight on my shoulders.

Couple this with just having my second child, and the joys of being self-employed with no maternity leave - I felt as though I had no other options. I had to just plod on, trying to be happy with a situation that on the outside, seemed like a dream career.

During this time, I did actually apply for and seriously consider taking a job outside the home, so I just wouldn't have to deal with the demands anymore. It was soul crushing, especially when the whole aim of my business was so I could work at home with my children. But it was too much, the projects were too much, I had too many clients.

I had been sucked into the trap of more, and I couldn't see a way out.

On The Other Side of More

Luckily for me, I did end up coming out the other side of the experience with a fresh take on the idea of 'more clients.' In experiencing it, I realized just how toxic the message of more was to a service provider. After the haze of post pregnancy hormones wore off and I saw clearly what the real issue was - my chasing of the idea of more clients - I knew I needed to put some constraints around this idea, in order to not get sucked back into it.

How do we put guidelines and constraints around this idea of more clients, so we're operating from a place of strength, rather than constantly trying to catch a bus that's pulling away five minutes early every damn day?

The first step is to put some guidelines around what the word 'more' means to us. More is intangible, fleeting. More has the soul-sucking power to never be fulfilled, because it's so vague. When you take the concept of more and replace it with clear constraints around what you can realistically provide by way of your services, it takes the power away from more and releases you from its hold.

More is unlimited, but when we know we only physically and mentally have the capacity for a certain number of clients, or a certain number of projects, more loses its hold and we can keep hold of our sanity.

Begin by sitting down and identifying how many hours a week you have to work on your client projects. Factor in things like sleep, rest, days off, and family time if needed. When I sat down and clearly wrote out how many hours per week I could conceivably work with my two children in tow, and my love of a normal sleep schedule, it turned out to be roughly 3-4 hours per day, and five on a day when the nap gods smiled on me. Multiplying this by five gave me between 15 and 20 hours per week I had to work on client projects, and in my business. Very short of what I would have needed to successfully serve the 12 clients I had taken on before then.

Once we know our own magic number, it becomes easier to say no to projects or schedule them later, so we're able to better serve them. Just like making sure we're on top of our schedule, this technique helps to beat back the more beast by setting the limits of what more means to us.

If we only have 20 hours a week to work on projects, then it serves to reason there is a limit to how many clients can fill those hours. When we know this data, we can shift that feeling of needing more into something that doesn't seem so intangible and fleeting.

Shifting From More to Better

Once we have the feeling of more constrained, we can start taking the next step of this process. Focusing on quality over quantity. From more to better.

If we know we only have so many hours per week to work on our projects and serve our clients, wouldn't it be better if we could serve fewer clients more fully, than rapidly hopping from project to project each day? For the vast majority of us, we've been kept under this spell of more clients for so long, we just keep looking for the next one and the next one - never stopping to think about how some of the most common business principles apply very much to us too.

In marketing and advertising, it's well known that it costs more money to acquire a new customer than it does to serve an existing one. Whole departments are devoted to reducing the churn rate for this very same reason. It stands to reason this would also apply to us as service providers, don't you think?

The more trap is seductive, and we often fall victim to the allure of bigger numbers, because they're sexy and give us the false illusion of our success. If we have served 100 clients - doesn't that seem better than serving 50?

What if instead of focusing on getting more or new clients, we instead redoubled our efforts to get existing clients to work with us again and again? What if we took those 50 clients and instead increased the average project size, and doubled the revenue from each one? In the end, the results would be the same, but we'd have far fewer clients to manage and the experience for both us serving them and them being served, would be far smoother and less hectic for everyone involved.

When you shift the lens to accepting clients based on quality rather than quantity, you start to make more money and decrease the time spent running around like a chicken with its head cut off. This simple shift in my own mindset allowed me to really see where I was undercharging, and how I could reduce the number of clients I was working with, while also seeing an increase, (or at least, not a decrease) in the revenue I was bringing in each month.

I started quoting more for my services, and the projects I bid on. I informed my existing clients the rates I charged two, three, or even five years ago would no longer apply. While scary at first, the vast majority had no problem with it. They were more than understanding about the cost of living changing in that time period. I had gotten far more skilled, and more often than not, I could finish the same project in at least 25% less time than when we first started working together.

It was a win-win situation for us all. Plus, it allowed me to realize which of my existing clients were quality and worth keeping, and which were not a good fit for me any longer; who perhaps were there because I hadn't vetted them more thoroughly.

Doing this consistently allows us to re-qualify our clients. It's a hard fact that the clients we worked with previously may not be a good fit for us anymore, and vice versa - we may be going in a direction with our services which doesn't suit their needs any longer.

This shift occurs for every service provider moving from hired gun to Secret Weapon - there are clients who simply hired us for a one-off project, or who thought of us as an expense and not an investment in their business. We can absolutely feel free to lovingly release those clients to find another provider who would be a better fit for their needs. It's not our job to change them and turn them around to this new way of working and showing up. If they don't jive, then they don't jive, and we can let them go.

This frees us to focus our efforts on finding the clients who do fit us perfectly. Because I guarantee you, for every client you have to let go, there are several more waiting in the wings who need your services, and need a Secret Weapon to help them badly.

Refocus on Your Schedule

Focusing on quality over quantity makes the most amount of sense for us as service providers, because there is a limit to the number of hours we can work in a day. We've talked about being aware of our schedule and not overbooking ourselves, and this knowledge also helps us to escape the allure of the more trap, because it focuses us to be very pragmatic of our time and energy, we have to serve any new clients.

By consistently remaining focused on our schedule, and our limitations in terms of how many clients we can serve, we can ignore the alluring siren call of getting more clients. Because let's face it, just because we sign more clients, doesn't mean we can actually serve them.

Whenever I feel the more trap reaching out to snare me, my heart feels like it's racing and I get lightheaded. I can feel the reaction in my body, and at first, I used to think this stress reaction was because I wasn't doing something right or I was failing somehow. Because if I was doing well, I wouldn't be stressed out right?

But I soon realized the racing feeling I had wasn't because I wasn't doing well, it was because I was feeling more stressed than usual - most likely because I had lost sight of my schedule, and was feeling out of control.

You might relate to this when you feel you don't know what's going on with your projects, (even though you probably have them well in hand). Or if you feel as though you have nothing coming up in your schedule and will be on the streets in a week (which is total bullshit, and you know there are more projects coming in). Even when you get a particularly rough piece of feedback, and you're convinced you're horrible at what you do (which honestly, if you've been doing this for any length of time, is most likely an overreaction).

All of these emotions are fodder for the more trap, and it can cause us to kick into overdrive, slam the accelerator to the floor, and drive as fast as we can for More Clients, USA. Which I have to say, is a shit town in a very bad county.

The regulator on these feelings is our schedule.

Always, always refocus back on your schedule to calm the feelings of overwhelm and get back into a place of feeling in control of what's going on. Redo the exercise of how many hours each week you have to work on your business, how many clients you feel comfortable serving at one time. This helps ground us in reality and calms those feelings of not enough the more trap feeds on.

When we do this exercise over and over again, (honestly, I've probably done this close to a hundred times by now), it helps give ourselves proof of the fact we are not, in fact, failing and we're doing very well, thank you very much. This proof is based on the number of hours we have to work on any given project for any given client.

Knowing we have such a specific amount of time to work on projects for our clients, it helps us say no to the more feeling of needing new clients. We can honor our schedule and give ourselves the margin to work properly on everything we take on. When you solidly know how many clients you can (and want) to serve, then the more clients trap becomes irrelevant, because even though more may sound enticing, you know it's not for you.

The more clients trap can be seductive, it can be alluring, and it can seem like the holy grail of fixing our problems. But in the end, it only serves to bring us bigger problems.

We're not able to serve our clients to the best of our ability, because we're managing too many projects at once. We don't do the best work we're capable of, because we've imposed such strict deadlines on ourselves, so we can finish fast and move onto the next project.

The biggest drawback to the more client trap is it perpetuates the idea that you're a hired gun. Because you're rushing through the work, because you're not performing as well, because you're not working to make your clients feel supported - they're left with the opposite impression we want when we're transitioning to becoming a Secret Weapon.

And above all else, the more client trap leaves us with an empty hole that just can't be filled. We can't define more, and so it's an endless chase for something we can't quantify. It causes us to stress the eff out, because we feel as though we're doing something wrong since the feeling of needing more just won't ever be satisfied.

Overall, the more client trap is something which takes a while to identify in yourself, and to make sure you put in checks and balances to combat every time it arises. It still gets me, even now, and I'm running with the assumption that this will continually plague all service providers until the day we hang up our shingle, and call it a day on our business. Our awareness of it, and having the tools at the ready to make sure we don't fall victim to it, will ensure that we have a much better overall working environment for us, and for our clients. It'll help us work towards becoming our client's Secret Weapon and raise the standard of work in what we do.

Next time you feel the more trap teaching out from the abyss, trying to snag your pant leg and drag you down, refocus on your goal of becoming a Secret Weapon - grab that schedule, and remind yourself you're bound to the Newtonian idea of space time, and kick the feeling of more in the face.

For me.

TL:DR

- There are millions of articles and how-to post online telling us how to get more clients as if it's the be-all and end-all of our business success. But this leads to the More Client Trap.
- A Secret Weapon doesn't pay attention to the notion that getting more clients will somehow be the solution to all their business worries.
- You can be just as successful serving fewer clients. Success and more clients do not go hand in hand.
- More clients is vague and undefined, and leaves us with feelings of inadequacy and being unfulfilled.
- Focus on quality clients rather than quantity. One client paying three times as much is twice as valuable as three clients.
- Realign yourself with your schedule, so you know exactly how many hours each week you have to serve your clients. You'll see that there is a limit to the number of clients you can reasonably serve.
- Escaping the more trap is a constant struggle for service providers, but awareness of how it presents itself in you is a key first step.

A SECRET WEAPON GROWS AS A PROVIDER

When I was in college, I took a diploma program called Digital Arts and Media. It was the first of its kind across Canada, and the program creator was known for being a bit of a wild child, a pioneer in the field of digital arts at the time. This was 2001, right at the time when people were beginning to see how the digital arts and careers within them were not only viable, but a smart decision for a young person to make.

I entered into this program not really knowing what to expect. Other than a brief description, which covered some of the topics we'd be learning, and a roster of very successful digital creators and business owners as teachers - there wasn't really much to go on, other than a gut feeling and a willingness to try it out.

At the time, I wanted to pursue a career in the arts - I liked creating, but I knew I probably wasn't going to be able to make a good living as a painter or sculptor. I liked the idea of a career using the advanced technologies I was starting to see all around me, and the program wasn't very expensive. In the end, I figured I had nothing to lose.

Little did I know at the time, that the program was an experiment.

Being the first of its kind, the program was created in such a way so we didn't have any choice in what topics we learned, or what fields we would specialize in. The degree was designed to give us a taste of everything we might need. It was designed to create digital generalists, jack of all trades with a computer.

Many of the people who went through the program failed to create a career from the skills we were taught. Many thought it was a waste of time and money. And when the program eventually was shut down two years after I graduated, they assumed their thoughts were well-founded. How could a program get shut down if it was a success?

But I think of it in a much different way. Yes, it didn't really prepare me for a specific career or job role. I didn't graduate with a degree in visual communications, and yet, I learned photography, multimedia design, and graphic design. I didn't have a certificate in computer science, and yet, I learned web design, html coding, and multimedia game creation. I didn't have a degree in film and video, and yet, I learned video editing, video production, audio engineering, and production planning.

I did earn a diploma in Digital Arts and Media - and the ability to pick and choose the type of career adventure I wanted, without being hemmed in by a particular job role or slice of the digital industry. I learned how to teach myself new concepts and skills quickly, focusing on the meat and expanding from there.

I learned how to grow.

Most of all, I discovered exactly how I would be running my career from that point on. Never pigeonholing myself in one specific industry, job title, or label. Always reaching, growing, and trying new things, without feeling as though I'd abandoned or had failed at what I was doing before.

Because in truth, the mindset was the key part of the program I took. It showed me that to excel in the digital arts, you had to be a bit of a jack of all trades and specialize in very few things. It showed me that a general knowledge was far more valuable than a specialized set of skills.

I look around at the job postings I see online, and the calls for help from business owners, and I see mirrored to me the mindset that program taught me are coming to fruition a few years later than they had originally planned.

Clients and business owners are needing digital generalists now more than ever, and as a digital service provider, you have to find the right balance of growing yourself and serving your customers. A groundbreaking, novel concept back in 2001, this is completely commonplace in 2019. The digital landscape, the technology we use, and the strategies we employ for our clients, are changing at a rapid pace - and we need to keep up.

Making sure this process of keeping caught up to the new changes in technology, systems, tools, and ways of working in our industry is hallmark of a Secret Weapon. In this section of the book, I'm going to be going through some key techniques and concepts, which I've found the best Secret Weapons use in their business, and for helping their clients. Some are concrete, and some are less so, but all are important to make sure you not only attain your Secret Weapon status but keep it for years to come.

KNOWING OUR LIMITS AS A PROVIDER

When I first graduated college in 2003, with my shiny new degree and the world ahead of me I knew I had three choices.

The first was to become a graphic designer and try to work in a design studio, print company, or agency of some sort. Start from the bottom and work my way up to maybe one day become a senior designer or an Art Director.

The second option was to go into audio and video production - I could become a camera person, editor, or a visual effects person who would probably work for peanuts at the start, but again, I'd work my way up to a more senior position in the company.

The third option I had was to strike out on my own and forge my own path. I had the skills from many different industries at that point, and could fit in or create a job, position, or title for myself.

I immediately scratched the third one off my list, because it was too scary, too daunting, and as I mentioned before in this book - I had absolutely no intention of working for myself or being an entrepreneur.

I ended up taking the first option. I started applying for graphic design positions in various industries and got hired at first a packaging company, then a print and silk-screening company, and afterwards a gym. In my mind, they were all forward moves - each job had more responsibility and paid more than the last, and I felt I was well on my way to creating a good career in the field of graphic design.

That all changed the day I was headhunted by a Fortune 500 oil company to be the design and development support in their training department. When they interviewed me, they asked me about all the other skills I had - of course, they could see I was a great graphic designer, but how was I at building websites? How was I at using online platforms? Could I create videos and edit together video footage? How about animations? Could I do tech support?

In that interview, I remember thinking back to my experimental schooling in college and nodding, yes, I did know how to do all of that. I just was a bit rusty on account of not doing much of it since graduation. It was the very first time I had been interviewed, and there was no clear-cut role or position for me. There was no succinct title. It was a little bit like the wild west, (only with far fewer shootings and way more money being paid each month).

So, I said yes. Yes, I absolutely can do all of this - and more! I thought back to my school classes and made up an even bigger list of the things I could do. The skills I had, (albeit a bit rusty), and the projects I had created in college which would apply to what they were doing in their department.

Little did I know that this was the start of a very slippery hill I would later find myself at the bottom of, wondering just how I had fallen so damn far.

After I left the oil company, I continued on this "just say yes" path for a number of years. I was always looking for more ways to bring what I thought were valuable services to my clients. I stretched and reached, and barely made it on some projects, because there were just a little past my working knowledge. I learned a ton, but I was stretched very thin, and I was always outside of my comfort zone.

One day, several years later, I woke up and realized my project list looked like the inside of a hoarder's closet. On the docket were three websites for various companies, the editing of several small videos for a personal trainer, the creation of a print brochure for a land developer, the writing of email copy for a client's welcome email campaign, and the creation of a course curriculum for a business coach teaching sales.

It was a hot mess. I was using every single skill I had, and not doing any of them all that well.

Initially, part of me thought the diversity was a good thing - I get to do so many different cool projects! It seemed exciting, varied, and different. But at the end of the day, I spent so much time switching between skills, back and forth on totally different projects, that I was left feeling exhausted and overwhelmed.

In this period of time, I learned a big lesson on my path to becoming a Secret Weapon, and it's helped shape how I view my projects and work with my clients ever since.

Knowing our strengths and our weaknesses, and only offering services aligned with our strengths is a hallmark of a Secret Weapon. It's no longer a matter of what we *can* do, but rather a matter of what we *should* do. We leave the tasks and projects we're only okay at to others who are stellar at them. We know the limits of our skills, and we stick to them.

By doing this, it helps us shape the services we offer to our clients. We can better ignore the content, courses, and shiny objects related to tasks or skills we've decided not to offer.

For me, this looks like focusing on the tech and design side of things. I focus on how they work and how they look. I don't worry about how they're launched. I don't think about the quality of the words used, and I don't do the video editing, sound engineering, animation, or any of the hundreds of other parts which could trip me up and make me lose focus.

Secret Weapons know their limits and their boundaries when it comes to the types of work they offer to their clients.

A One Person Shop

If you do a search on Pinterest for online business services, you'll get a gajillion posts with lists of the many different services you can offer to be 'more valuable' to potential clients. List posts of 65+ services which will make our clients hire us seem to be popping up all over the place - and it's incredibly detrimental to the average service provider just trying to do work they love, for clients who respect them, and they love working with.

In the search for being able to add more value to the services we provide, we end up becoming even less valuable, because we confuse our clients as to what exactly we do.

When I first left the oil company, I made the mistake of listing out the laundry list of skills and knowledge I had, thinking clients would see these diverse range of skills as perfect for what they were looking for.

I assumed since I was a unicorn, possessing all these different skills, clients were indeed looking for someone who could handle it all. The same holds true for many different online service providers I see - especially the field of virtual assistants. Because a virtual assistant's work is so varied, they mistakenly believe they need to offer everything, in order to prove themselves valuable to their potential clients.

Often, this leaves us doing the work we don't enjoy or aren't skilled enough at. This causes frustration, burnout, and late nights trying to figure out small nuances of a skillset we've dabbled with but aren't experienced enough, to take on more complex jobs.

Cassidy, a single mother who decided to work online after having her second child, told me about how she felt pressured to offer a wide range of services. She said the height of those feelings came after she watched a webinar talking about how by offering a laundry list of over 18 services, she could make more money than the average virtual assistant online.

"I felt like in order to make any sort of money, those were the services I had to offer - even though I didn't have any experience in things like video editing and Facebook ads. I had one client who I offered Facebook advertising services to, and I lost her a bunch of money because I just honestly had no idea what I was doing. I was so stressed out for the entire project that at the end of it, I had to cancel on the client and say I just couldn't do it anymore."

Cassidy is only one of the many service providers I talked to who felt as though they really needed to offer all these services in order to be successful and help their clients. The idea that they could only offer one or two services, and thrive doing just those, seemed foreign and akin to a wonderful fairy tale.

This feeling of having to do everything, of needing to have as many different services as possible, stems from one big issue I see many potential Secret Weapons suffer from: the inability to work from their strengths.

Strengths vs Niches

If you've been working in the online space or have read any sort of marketing-related information source, then I'm assuming you've heard of the very popular term - niching down.

The concept is not new, nor is it novel. Picking a niche and sticking to it has been used as general business advice for a very long time. Though many people get confused as to what it applies to.

Does it apply to the people you serve or the services you offer? From my perspective, it's a little bit of both. On one hand, we need to be able to succinctly describe what we do and what we don't do - and on the other, we need to be able to know who we're looking to work with, and who we don't want to work with.

Niching down has two purposes. First, it helps us avoid the very real trap of trying to offer every service under the sun and secondly, it lets us define who we are most wanting to work with. This lets us target our marketing and client acquisition efforts towards a smaller group of people, usually with more success.

In the case of becoming a Secret Weapon, we're going to focus on the former - niching down our services and offerings, so we're able to focus exclusively on the things *we* want to do, the things we're good at, and bring us the most amount of satisfaction.

Rather than call it a niche, we're going to call it our strength. And of course, we should play to our strengths, right?

When we focus on our strengths and what we actually want to be doing, it gets a lot easier to find clients who want to pay us for doing just that. We're not trying to offer 65 different services. We're able to clearly communicate what we do, the value we bring, and how we're the best logical choice.

It's far more powerful when we're able to distill down what we do into a few words title than a vague description of what we can help with.

Rather than being a Virtual Assistant, you can become a client care specialist. Rather than a web developer, you can become an eCommerce developer. Instead of a graphic designer, you can become a packaging designer.

I can tell you this helps tremendously when being looked for and getting hired by potential new clients. Clients and business owners looking to fill a role or get a project done are looking for specific skill sets. They're not hiring for a graphic designer slash video editor slash bookkeeper slash social media manager; they're looking for one of those things. When we broadcast our expertise in all these things, a client is left confused as to what we're actually *good* at.

When we play to our strengths, we not only get more clients looking for specific things, but we get to work on the projects we enjoy, rather than trying to fulfill projects we don't like, or struggle with.

Defining Your Strengths

Knowing that we need to play to our strengths and acknowledging we need to niche down in our offerings is one thing - but finding those strengths, and defining our niche is totally different. If not done correctly, it can cost us valuable credibility with our clients, and lost opportunities when marketing our services.

When I first heard about the concept of niching down, I took it entirely too far. I was working primarily as a web developer after leaving the oil company, and generally getting by. There were ups and there were downs, but for the most part, I was doing pretty good.

Then I read a bunch of books on the concept of niching down, and it fueled this idea in me that I could become a specialist in a part of the market where I saw very few experts or providers in - the online course industry.

I had lots of real-world experience in instructional design, so the move seemed like a no brainer for me. I researched the competition, liked what I saw in terms of the viability of the market, and made the decision to start offering course creation, course design, and course auditing services.

I dove in headfirst, and created an entirely new brand, a new company focused primarily on online course creation and services. When I did this, it was essentially akin to starting over. I had become known for doing design and web development services up until this point, so the switch to online courses left my current clients scratching their heads as to if I could still serve them.

I tried to balance both companies at the same. On the one hand, I was still serving my existing clients doing one thing, yet I was advertising a totally different set of services to new prospects.

While I did gain traction in the online course business, it took me quite some time to start making a name for myself in that space and it was a hard, uphill battle. After a year and a half of not much progress, I came to the realization I had taken the niching down advice too far. Instead of applying it in the right way - by playing to my strengths - I had started something I regretted and would later fold back into my original business.

If I had gone about it the right way, I feel I would have seen much faster success, and not had to overcome the inevitable loss of clients and confusion, because they just weren't sure what I was doing anymore, and which company they were working with.

What I should have done was to keep my existing company and branding intact, and simply offered a branch of services aligned with course creation. Since course creation and instructional design was one of my strengths, it was complementary to what I was doing at the time. I would have saved myself a lot of time and energy working on creating a new brand, a new company, and dividing my attention between two different businesses.

After I realized my mistake, I sat down and decided to refocus my services and offerings based on my strengths. I made a list of approximately eight services I enjoyed doing, and knew I was very good at.

From this list of services, I identified my key core areas, which boiled down to design, marketing tech implementation, and online course tech implementation.

I now had three well defined categories aligned with what I knew my strengths to be. It was an immense relief to say I only offered these things going forward and freed up a lot of my brain power when it came to new clients asking for services I didn't offer, because the answer was no - sorry!

Finding Your Ideal Services

How do we define our own strengths in order to offer services we're good at, enjoy doing, and are capable of creating results for our clients with?

It's tempting to follow every new list post on Pinterest or the web with what services we *should* be offering, and to expand our list to include as many as possible. But this is going to run us ragged and stall our forward momentum.

I want to outline for you a simple set of guidelines, which helped me shape the services and skills I offer to my own clients and have helped me ignore most of the advice floating around the internet as to what I should or should not offer.

The first part of this is determining clear delineation between fields we can use to see where our strengths lie, and where we're able to offer the most value to our clients. By segmenting the skill sets or strengths we already have, we're able to see where they fall into these broad categories, and base future decisions on our conclusions.

There are four main categories, or areas most service providers fall into. True Secret Weapons know which ones they're strongest in and stick to them - they don't venture too far outside of their categories, because they know it's a waste of their precious time and attention.

Hired guns tend to jump back and forth, weaving their way through all four, hoping to catch attention based on how versatile they are, when in fact, they're doing the opposite and weakening their clients' perception of them and their skills.

These four categories, like most disciplines, aren't set with concrete walls between them. There is overlap and most skills and services draw from more than one category. The point of this categorization isn't to fit everything into neat little boxes, but to instead come up with a very strong perception of where our strengths lie, where we're weakest, and where we're just not passionate about something.

This categorization is designed to save us time and effort moving forward in our business and focusing on bringing the best value possible, rather than diluting our offerings over time.

Alright, so that being said, what are these four categories?

They are:
- Design
- Technology
- Growth
- Operations and Admin

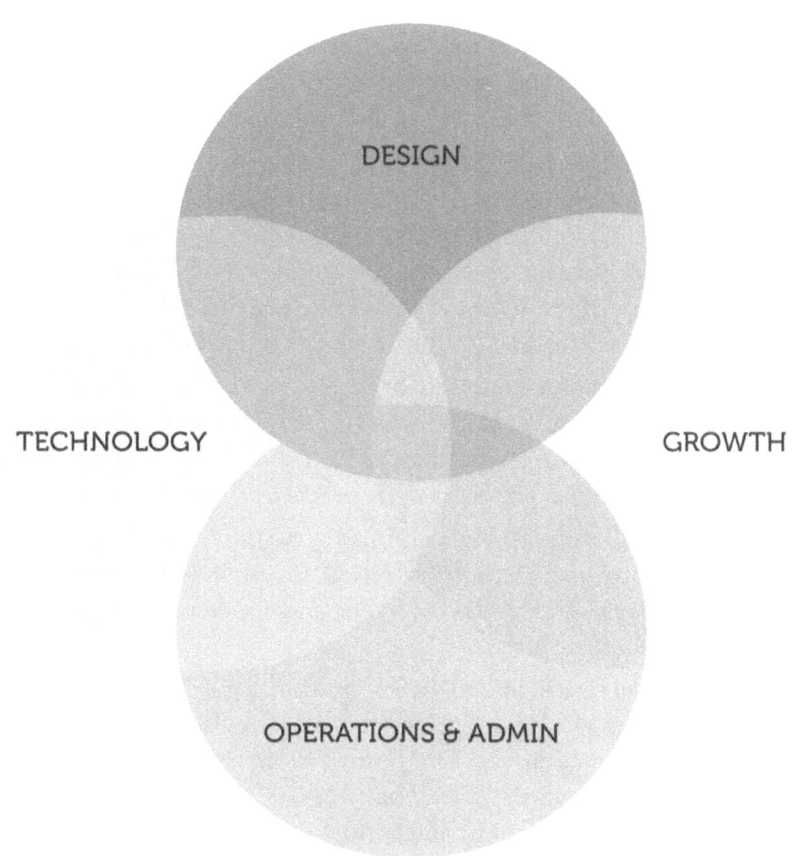

As you're looking at those categories, you're thinking to yourself - wow those are broad, I have services spanning all four! And you'd be totally correct. Like I mentioned before, very rarely are there services which fall smack dab in the middle of one specific category, most of them straddle the lines between two or even combine elements of all four - but knowing which of these categories you're particularly strong in will help you avoid the need to offer services in the categories you aren't.

Design

Design is the category everyone wants to be good at. I would say this category is the most pervasive, leaching into many different services, and lending a hand to support so many offerings. But, design is also the one category that when it's not one of our strengths, we can seriously overcommit ourselves, and tax our resources trying to make it work.

Many people mistakenly believe design is a natural talent - you're either born with it or not. But just like being able to draw, paint, or sculpt, design is not about natural talent, but rather about practice and application. When I first started my college program in Digital Arts and Media, I would never have called myself an artist or designer by any stretch of the word. I *wanted* to be one, yes, but other than a few high school art classes, I never really devoted my time or energy to practice how to draw, learn what what makes up a good composition, or many of the other factors which come into play when it comes to art and design.

But over the years, and through many, many hours of practice, I started getting really good. Now, it's by far one of the strongest categories in my own skill set. If you've seen my website, my promotional materials, or any of my free resources, I designed every one of them. Since it's one of my categories, I make full use of those strengths where I can.

If you're strong in the design field, then you most likely are pulled towards the industries of graphic or web design. You see how things could look better, and you acknowledge when something seems 'off' about designs you see online or in print.

If you're strong in the design category, the services you're most likely to be the best at are graphic design, image creation, web design, branding, and visual representations for your clients. These tasks light you up, and you enjoy them immensely. You love color, fonts, and layouts. Using tools like Canva, Photoshop, Illustrator, and other design programs feels comfortable to you.

Technology

The technology category has the most potential to earn a higher hourly wage, and help you become more sought after for your work. The technology category is about adaptability, and being good at intuitively being able to figure out new ways of doing things online.

It's also the category where the most self doubt lives. It's the one where we're constantly second guessing ourselves, and it's where the majority of service providers throw up their hands and say they, 'just don't get it.'

Technology guides the infrastructure and initiatives of many online businesses, and being able to use and adapt to new technology is the mark of a tech-strong Secret Weapon.

Some of the main features of a tech-strong Secret Weapon include being able to quickly apply patterns from use of other programs to new software. Quickly being able to figure out a new piece of software, and weighing its capabilities and limitations based on the final end result or goals.

Being strong in the tech category doesn't mean you're an expert in one type of software or platform, but rather flexible enough to use various platforms, depending on what your clients desired goals are. It means you're comfortable breaking things and figuring out how they work and connect to each other, and it usually means you're okay with not knowing everything upfront and figuring it out in the end.

If your strength lies in the technology field, then you're curious about how new platforms and software can fit into an existing strategy, or tactics for your clients. You most likely spend a portion of your time learning new systems, new features, new ways of using technology and systems, to achieve the end results your clients are looking for.

Growth

Being strong in the growth category is akin to being a strategist. The service providers I know who are strongest in this category are the ones most focused on overall strategies rather than individual tactics. They love marketing and optimization, and focus on providing solutions that meet an end goal of business growth for their clients, rather than any one specific task.

If you're strong in the growth category, you're most likely a great writer, a great planner, and can see how day to day efforts and techniques combine to create an end result greater than the whole. Many service providers who are growth focused tend to focus on services like marketing and advertising, sales funnel creation, online courses and other business growth tools designed to get their client from point A to point B.

Growth focused service providers are the ones who generally don't identify themselves as service providers, but rather strategists and experts. They focus on the results they get for their clients, and don't spend much energy on the specific details of how they get there. Not to say they don't care about or do those specific action steps, but rather that's not what they're selling to their clients. They know their clients aren't as interested in the specific task list which gets them there, only that they arrive safe and sound, reaching their business goals.

Service providers who are strong in the growth category are very focused on learning. In order to be able to provide their customers with new and updated strategies and tactics, they are very quick to identify and follow new trends and spend a lot of time testing and figuring out new methods of putting those strategies into place.

Many sales funnel specialists, social media managers, advertisers, and marketing focused service providers are very strong in the growth field. In my experience, the growth category is one in which, the farther distance you have from the other categories, the more potential you have for becoming less of a hands-on service provider, and more of a consultant.

Operations and Admin

The operations and admin category is where service providers who excel at the seemingly small, consistent tasks really excel. Secret Weapons, who specialize in admin are incredibly detail oriented and don't mind working on the relatively mundane tasks that go into running a business.

Admin category tasks include things like managing email, client administration, business reporting, personal scheduling, and business analytics. These aren't very glamorous tasks but bring with them a high level of satisfaction for the right type of person.

The admin field is where I struggle personally, so in my business, I offer no services that align with this category - but that's just me.

Perhaps you're an admin rockstar who excels at taking on these small, consistent tasks and knocking them out of the park. Perhaps reports are your peanut butter and jam and you love answering customer support tickets. If bookkeeping and data entry are in your wheelhouse, then there are very few businesses who don't need people like you.

While not as glamorous as some of the other categories, the admin category is by far the largest and most important for the average business owner. You'll find far more job postings and clients needing work done along the lines of admin based work than you will for any of the other categories.

The Truth About Specialization

If there's one thing I've noticed throughout my career and with working with other service providers is there's a phenomenon I call the specialization conundrum.

There is a direct correlation between where you sit on the category venn diagram, and how much money you can reasonably charge for your services. The service providers who are close to the middle of the diagram, meaning their strengths overlap greatly between the categories, tend to be generalists. They can do a bit of everything, and easily find themselves doing work from all four of the major categories, depending on the project, the client, and how they feel that month.

Other service providers are way out at the fringes of a specific category, and don't straddle the lines at all. They're specialists and focus primarily on one or two services which are very distinct and specialized for their field. These are service providers who don't like straying from their comfort zone too much and make it very clear to everyone they only do a certain thing, and they do it very well.

There is a direct correlation between where you sit on this sliding scale and the amount of money you earn. The specialists make far more money per hour on average than generalists, and are able to either further specialize or refine the projects they work on, so they can be more picky about who and what they're working on at any given point.

But the inverse of this is, generalists tend to get more projects and more clients because they're more adaptable to the specific needs, and are able to offer a wide variety of services.

There is no right or wrong way about their correlation though. It's simply a sliding scale you need to be aware of. Would you like to stay a generalist and be able to serve more people, but perhaps make a bit less money per project? Or would you rather be a specialist who works with fewer clients, but earns more money per project on average?

I know a lot of service providers who have struggled with this decision in the past. Choosing a few categories to focus your skills, service, and energy and from there further refining and specializing your skills can be a hard decision for anyone to make. Do you stay a generalist? Do you specialize?

Ultimately, this is a decision you'll have to make for yourself, but I do want to save you some unwanted frustration by saying it's almost impossible to be great in all four of these categories. The best Secret Weapons straddle two of them, and none of them try to provide services in all four.

Think now on how you can streamline your service offerings to include services from your top strengths. Work within your boundaries, and set limits of what you can and cannot do for your clients. Be clear on what you offer, and avoid the shiny object syndrome of offering a service just because 'it's hot right now.' Not only will you be much happier, but it'll help you more clearly communicate what you do and the value you bring to your prospective customers, now and in the future.

TL:DR

- Trying to say yes to every single project or service you could possibly provide is a sure way to get yourself a one-way ticket to burnout.
- Secret Weapons focus on offering services aligned to their strengths and skill sets rather than 'what's hot right now' in the business world.
- By eliminating the distraction of offering all the services, you not only make it easier to communicate your value, but clients are immediately clear on how you can help them.
- There are four main categories amongst service providers, almost all skills or services fall into various combinations of the four:
    o Design
    o Technology
    o Growth
    o Operations and Admin
- There's almost always overlap in between these four, but the more overlap there is in your services, the more generalized you are.
- Specialists are further out on the edges of the categories and have less overlap in their services, so they tend to be able to charge more money to work with them.
- Generalists are able to accept far more jobs than specialists, so they have no shortage of clients, but tend to be able to charge less per hour.
- The sliding scale exists, it's your choice on where you sit on that scale.

PRODUCTIZING OUR SERVICES

What's the difference between a home cooked meal and dinner at a restaurant? Besides the obvious addition of love, what truly sets them apart?

If you cook anything like me, then the answer is the meal cooked at home is custom made. Maybe you followed a general recipe, but in the end, the exact specifications weren't set in stone. You may have added extra ingredients that you felt would complement it, and the sides just sort of came together based on what you had in the pantry.

By comparison, the meal made in a restaurant follows a very specific formula, time and time again in order to maximize flavor, experience, presentation, and the cost to the restaurant to produce.

Which of these is the better meal?

Neither of them is better than the other - they're just two very different ways of preparing food to get you to the end results - a nice meal you can enjoy.

For years, the work I did was the home cooked meal. It was custom, bespoke, and tailored specifically to each and every client I worked with. Every project was different, even though the end results were almost identical when things were said and done.

I started each project with a blank slate, built it from the ground up, and customized it to suit the client's needs and end goals. There was nothing inherently wrong with that, by no means was it a bad way to go.

But it took a lot of work.

Each project I completed somehow always overextended it's scope, ran through it's timelines, and ended up being much more work than I originally thought it would be. One day I sat down, and decided I needed to figure out what the issue was. There had to be a reason why these projects were running off the rails so often, even though by all standards, they were run of the mill websites or marketing projects, which should have been fairly straightforward.

What I found was the majority of the work I did was not, in fact, custom. It was the same thing over and over again, and by approaching it in this bespoke, custom manner, I was adding unnecessary work to every project I worked on.

With this discovery, I set out to more clearly outline my projects - the recipes I used - to create the end results my clients wanted. Creating set lists and items for deliverables, identifying key components which could be reused from project to project, and making the scope of each project more streamlined in the execution.

During this time, I came across a fellow who was talking about productizing services. Essentially, making your services as close to a product as possible so you can easily recreate them, (and the results they bring to your clients).

Brian Casel changed my life at the most opportune time, and I highly recommend you look him up for further resources on this topic.

Using his teachings on the topic, I was able to streamline my production and offer my services in a way that made sense for me doing the work and made sense for my clients purchasing them. Because when you think about it - everything about creating custom work is harder.

Custom is Harder to Create

As service providers, everything we do tends to be thought of as custom work. We see it through the lens of originality and creativity, and so the patterns between projects can be hard to see when we're so engrossed in doing the work. But when we're examining each client's individual needs and responding with a solution made specifically to their situation, it takes far more work.

At first, we love the idea of custom work, we're free to tailor our services to the client's needs and we can offer something which fits like a well-made tailored suit. It empowers us to have more control over the process, and the results we see from doing this kind of work helps to reinforce the idea that this is the way to go.

There are so many other parts of our business we gladly rinse and repeat. We reuse the same contracts, the same invoices, and we certainly don't create a brand-new style of working with each project we take on. Why then do we cling so hard to make everything we do a custom piece of work?

Perhaps it's our pride. Perhaps it feels as though if we were to offer something to a client that wasn't custom, it would somehow take away from our expertise or make us less talented. I think the main cause is that we feel that if we don't create everything ourselves, piece by piece, lovingly handcrafted each and every time, we will somehow lose control.

But when we're constantly having to reinvent the wheel for every project we work on, there's very little by way of predictability. We often feel less in control, and by the end, ready to be done with it completely. When everything we create for our projects is custom, it increases the workload by at least double. Having to create everything from scratch every time, even if we're incredibly good at what we do, is not only hard, but it's inefficient. And when you're a Secret Weapon, efficiency needs to be the name of the game. Not because we're trying to churn out massive amounts of projects for the bottom line, but because to do so otherwise, leads us down the path to burnout and dissatisfaction with the work we're doing.

When a service provider gets burned out, this leads to unhappy clients, hits to our reputation and let's face it - it just sucks for everyone involved. By flipping the script on custom work, and acknowledging yes, there are some things we do that are custom for each project, but the majority of the work is repeatable from project to project, we put in place stop-gaps to prevent burnout from happening in the first place, and we reduce the amount of work.

Custom is Harder to Manage

Custom projects are harder to keep control of the reins. When I was examining why the majority of my projects went off the rails and overran their time, budget, or scope, it led me to believe I was the problem - was I unable to stick to a timeline? Did I create unnecessary work? Was I the one who was undercharging for my services?

And the truth is that yes, I was - on all of those accounts. But it wasn't because I had any lack of skill, or I was bad at project managing, it was because I was approaching my projects from a stance of knowing what went into the project, but not taking into account having to create everything from the ground up. I was selling myself short, time and time again.

When we don't have clear guidelines around the amount of time it takes us to do a specific type of project, and what resources we need to accomplish it, it leaves us suffering in the pricing department, and trying to make up for it in other departments - like quality or timelines.

When we make compromises in our deliverables, because we misunderstood the amount of work in a specific type of project, we ultimately suffer in our revenue. Very rarely do I see a service provider overcharging for a project, that ended up being less work than they thought it would be. Far too often, I see service providers working for what amounts to be half or a third of what they need to earn per hour, in order to survive.

But when we have clear guidelines around our projects, we're better able to manage our timelines, and know exactly how long a project of this type takes us to complete. We're better able to predict what the cost will be to us in terms of time and resources. This helps us bill more realistically and set project pricing that doesn't make us wince when we get paid.

Custom is Harder to Sell

Custom work is so very hard to market and sell. How many inquiries have you gotten that end with the catch-all service provider answer: "It depends, I'll need some more information."

This answer wears us down over time doesn't it? We feel helpless not being able to provide these very basic answers to prospective clients about price, timeline, and deliverability, without having to sit down for an hour-long conversation, before they've even decided if they want to go ahead with something like that.

It's a waste of our time. Since we are solely dependent on our time as a means to put food on the table, and keep us in Apple products, that time can't be wasted on doing a deep dive into a client's needs, when we aren't even sure if we can offer them something to meet their goals.

When every project we create is custom, it becomes so much harder to talk about with our prospects and our clients. Trying to describe a brand-new painting, when brush hasn't been put to canvas, is almost impossible for an artist and so too in our work, does this plague us.

We can grab examples and samples from here and there and say, "it will be like this, but different," and this hurts us in our sales process rather than helping. We need to be able to clearly express the exact features, the exact benefits, and the exact end product the client will be getting. We need to paint the picture beforehand, rather than relying on our client's imagination filling in the blanks and deciding it's worth it.

When we productize or package our services in such a way as to make them clear and concise for the client looking to work with us, we're taking a lot of the hard work out of the process for them. It becomes easier to talk about the work we do, because we have clear boundaries about what's included and what's not. And above all else, it helps us get over that dreaded, "it depends," scenario where we can't give our clients any real answers unless we sit down with them for an hour to pick their brain.

Going the route of productizing our services allows us to clearly own the outcomes of our projects even further, because we know all the variables going into the project in the first place.

The Process of Productizing Your Services

The act of packaging up what we do into nice neat little piles can seem daunting at first. We don't know where to start, what to focus on, and what makes the most sense from the viewpoint of our customers. We also tend to think it precludes us from offering anything else outside of these set packages. All of this can prevent us from starting.

Instead of thinking we're no longer able to provide these other services, view it instead as top and eye-level shelves in a supermarket. When a person goes into a supermarket, it's been designed to put the most common and highest selling items at eye level. The shelves are designed in such a way as to make it easy for someone to find what they need, and usually, this means they're looking for something pretty standard. But the supermarket doesn't lock away the rest of their products in a vault where you need a secret code word to get in, they just put them a bit further up, or a bit further down in the shelves, because they know statistically you're not looking for those items with the same frequency as you are the ones on the eye-level shelves.

So too with our packages. We're not hiding away the custom services, we're not locking them in a vault. We're just putting them above or below eye level. They're still there, but we're far more focused on the easier to sell, easier to explain services and packages we have.

When we look at it this way, it becomes a bit less constricting for us, and we can uncomplicate it so much more.

At the heart, productizing our services means creating set packages with specific details of what's offered, what's not offered, and how it rolls out in application to a client's business. We're able to confidently say package X does Y, and package Y does Z, because we know everything contained in both packages, and how they differ from one another.

Go through the services you offer the most frequently to clients. I'm sure you can see there are items which are more popular and get your clients better results than others. These will be your core packages. In my case, the most popular packages I have are my website package, and my marketing automation package. These are my bread and butter, and it's what I focus the most on when I talk to clients.

From there, you can feel free to split them into smaller or more custom packages. In my case, I have a website redesign package, a website from scratch package, and an all in one website package, combined with my marketing automation package. Based on their goals, I can usually tell which one would be the best fit for them, and which variation of the package would suit them best.

Having a set of 4-6 packages does wonders for our business, because it takes the guesswork out of what we sell, and how best to sell it. It gives us structure around what we're creating, and how we create it, giving us space to bring in things like automations, frameworks, templates, and more to further support the project, so we don't feel as though we're starting from scratch with every new client we sign on.

When we create packages like this and have them clearly outlined, we can draw clear boundaries around what is expected of us, what is expected of the client, the deliverables, and the timelines required.

Outlining Your Packages

When we have our packages created, and we're sure they give the best value to our clients, we can then move on to providing structure to them internally.

The four major components of any productized service are:
1. The deliverables
2. The timelines
3. The outcomes
4. The follow-up

The Deliverables

What exactly is your client going to get from this project? When we're all finished, what will they be left with in terms of assets, features, and tangible items from our work? When we lay out the exact deliverables of a project, it becomes so much harder for the projects to enter into scope creep territory. If it doesn't have a home on this list, then it is outside the scope of the project, period.

We can, of course, alter the deliverables here and there to ensure our package is meeting our clients needs, but when we take the time to clearly set out the project deliverables, there are no misunderstandings in the process.

When creating our list of deliverables for a project, we want to keep it confined to the cold, hard facts. It can be easy to pepper in marketing speak here to make these deliverables seem more attractive. Avoid the temptation to do so.

Don't offer promises in this list of deliverables. This can mean the difference between having a landing page on your list of deliverables, vs. a landing page that converts at a certain guaranteed percentage. Keep the results of your deliverables out of your list, and you'll save yourself tons of headaches down the road.

The Timelines

Next up in your project outline should be the timeline. Since you have a very defined list of the deliverables each project entails, you can clearly tell how long it's going to take you to deliver those to your client. Be generous with yourself here, and make sure to build in a 5-10% margin to ensure you have room to spare for when things go awry, or if a client is slow to communicate with you.

Break down the project into distinct phases, and determine the approximate timelines for each phase. This helps us not only plan better for our own scheduling, but it will ensure we communicate to our client the distinct parts of the project, and when they'll be completed.

No client has ever complained about a project being completed early, but there are horror stories in abundance of service providers not giving themselves enough time to deliver, and missing the deadlines they initially promised.

Don't be one of those service providers, and make sure the timelines you create for each of your projects take into account the work being done, the client providing feedback, revisions, and that you'll most likely be working on other projects as well during this time.

The Outcomes

Here's where we get to pull out some of our marketing speak, and talk up the project a bit more. In the outcomes section, we're going to focus on the benefits of our package, not the features. What does having this completed project mean for them? Does it mean less time managing a certain part of their business? Does it mean having solid assets to reuse easily for their company? Does it mean that their customers will be better informed about the work they do? Or does it mean they won't have to feel frantic in the morning when they check their email?

Highlight these benefits in your outcomes as the most common side effects of having this project completed by yourself. Feel free to talk yourself up here, and use real world data from past clients projects to support your claims.

The key part of this is to base our outcome claims on average past results only, not on best case scenarios. We've all heard the claims from service providers about how their one client made $45,000 in one month from their project, when in reality the rest of their clients see an average of $2,000-$3,000. Don't be that person.

Yes, absolutely talk about the one client who got that amazing result, or the project you created that went on to do amazing things, but don't mislead your prospects by insinuating every project you create will end up with these great big results. By avoiding this, you'll allow your prospect to have a more realistic view of the project outcomes, and will take the pressure off of you to deliver these results time and time again. We all want to have amazingly successful projects we can highlight to everyone who can listen, but in my experience, it's the service provider who can create 100 projects with consistent results who close more deals, than the one who creates five projects with big results and 95 with less than stellar outcomes.

The Follow-up

Once the project is complete - what then? Having a portion of our project outline devoted to what comes after a project is a key part of making sure our clients feel cared for.

Do you offer maintenance or a support period? Do you have a guarantee that covers a certain amount of time after the project is completed? Explain these parts of your work, so you can be sure to talk about them when you're in a sales call with a prospect. Clients want to feel supported throughout every stage of the process, and by letting them know that once a project is finished, you aren't going to up and disappear, is going to make your packages much more attractive to anyone interested in working with you.

Systems and Frameworks for Completing Your Productized Services

Once we have the overall outline of our packages in place, they become easier to systemize and automate. We can examine what we can do to make them easier to complete. Whether those are templates or frameworks, SOP documentation, or even hiring someone else to do portions of the project.

When I did this in my own work, I ended up creating frameworks and templates for each type of project and saved about eight to ten hours for each one. I identified key assets so I could reuse them, created templates that could be transferred from client to client, and even set up a repeatable to-do list to guide me through the process each time, so I wouldn't have to sit down and wonder "what's next?"

Productivity is a huge word these days - we all want to be more productive. We chase time hacks and techniques to make us more productive in our work and in our businesses, but we often miss the mark, because when everything we do is custom work, there's no way to truly streamline.

Taking the custom portion out of the equation doesn't constrict us - it frees us to work within a defined set of boundaries where we can play. Creating templates to guide our process, frameworks to light the path forward, and operating procedures we can use to ensure we're always on track, will give us more, not less.

Sit down and go through your packages. Where can you create something to help you finish this project faster or with fewer man hours? What do you find yourself creating again and again for each project?

It could be as simple as a predetermined file structure, or as complex as a website framework. My friend Amanda, a copywriter who works primarily with health and wellness coaches, created a template within her writing program that she can easily bring up for every new project she works on. In it she captures the client's past messaging, information on their target market, links to their important pieces online, and testimonials her client has received in the past. Having those pieces already gathered and organized for her before she sits down to write the emails or the sales pages, ensures she has exactly what she needs at her fingertips, so she doesn't waste time searching for something she needs in the moment.

Increasing Profitability With Productized Services

Creating these assets and processes will do wonders for your profit margins. If you're able to get back five to ten hours of your time from each project, while still charging the same rate - where would that time be better spent? You could use it to acquire new clients, you could use it to promote your own business, and you could use it to give yourself the much needed margin to keep you rested, inspired, and ready to serve your clients to your highest capacity.

You'll get an increased number of clients who say yes to your projects when you approach them in this manner. Not only can you see exactly which type of project would suit them best, you'll be able to clearly explain what the project entails for them at each step of the way.

This leads to a much easier yes on the part of your prospects. They see clearly what the project entails, what they get out of it, and will feel far more comfortable saying yes to something when they know all the details. No one goes to buy a car without knowing exactly what they'll get - and in our work, we shouldn't be so concerned with ensuring everything we do is custom work. Because the truth of the matter is, you're most likely undercharging for that custom work. When you create packages of your services, you're much more likely to price them accordingly and allot for the real time spent, plus the knowledge and skill needed to complete them.

I encourage you to start this process within your own business. The less time it takes you to do the same work, the more time you're able to devote to acquiring new or repeat clients. You'll easily become the Secret Weapon for a group of clients who love what you do, because they know exactly what they're getting each time they work with you.

You'll start to see a decrease in the amount of time spent on each project you undertake, you'll see an increase in your conversion rate when talking to prospects about what you can do, and you'll see an overall upswing in the profitability of your business.

But overall - and this has been the most amazing by-product of adjusting the way I work in this manner - is that you'll have peace of mind when it comes to the outcomes of your projects.

When I was quoting 100% custom work, it was so hard to invest myself in the outcome of a project. I knew I could do my part, but the feeling that the project was going to fail because of some great unknown I would discover later, plagued me throughout the process. It was like a dark hammer above my head and I never knew if or when it would drop.

Once I set out clear outlines of what my projects did, what they contained, and the benefits they could bring, I was far more certain these projects would in fact, achieve the final outcomes. This freed me just that much more to be confident in the outcomes I could achieve for clients. It allowed me to become far more invested in those outcomes, because they were so much better defined.

We don't want to let our clients down, and when we're able to know with certainty our projects can achieve what we say they will, it allows us to step fully into the role of Secret Weapon, and leave the hired gun, custom work mentality behind that can trip us up or plague our confidence.

TL:DR

- Service providers tend to treat everything we do as custom work, which makes every project harder to complete and harder to communicate.
- Productizing our services means to create set packages with clear boundaries around what is contained and not contained within them.
- A packed or productized service has these main features:
    - Set deliverables
    - Set timelines and phases
    - Specific outcomes
    - Defined follow up
- When you know these components of each project, you're better able to create systems, frameworks, templates, and procedures to support you in delivering them faster and easier.
- Productized services are easier to sell to your prospects, because they know exactly what a project entails, this leads to greater profitability for your business because you'll get more yeses.
- The surprising side effect of having productized services is more confidence in what you create, and the outcomes that can be achieved, which lets you become more invested in the outcome of a project because they're clearly defined.

THE VALUE OF INVESTING IN OURSELVES

Investing is a funny word.

We think of investing as something bankers or brokers do, and our immediate thoughts are of the stock market and Wall Street. Men in business suits, making important deals for large sums of money. The hustle and bustle of the international markets and being able to decipher financial bond return values over the lifetime value of the commodity market (huh?).

Likely that didn't make much sense, because the typical reaction to the word investing brings out a lot of baggage and past assumptions in many people, especially those who trade their time for money.

Service providers are a special breed of people, who I've found have a resistance to the idea of investing. I've felt this resistance very strongly in my lifetime, and I believe it comes from the ingrained mindset which comes from earning a specific dollar amount for every task, every project, and every hour we work.

The idea of investing is so very different than what we're used to, we often shy away from it or don't believe it applies to us until we're thinking of saving or growing our retirement fund.

Our ideas when it comes to financial investing, and our preconceived notions about how it does and does not apply to our particular situation, greatly colors how we perceive the notion of investing in ourselves.

When I first started working freelance after leaving the oil company, I understood and was familiar with the trading of dollars for hours mentality. It was very much ingrained in me. As I started teaching myself about running an actual business, and came across the idea of a business investment, I was incredibly uncomfortable with what it presented to me.

An investment to me was risky. There was no guarantee if I purchased a specific piece of software or participated in a certain training course there would be any real payoff from it. There was no real time in = dollars out equation I could rely on to make sure it was worth it.

So, I naturally shied away from investing in myself, or my business, unless I absolutely had to for those first two years.

If I needed to figure something out, I would hit the research decks hard. I would Google like a queen, and while it sometimes took me hours, I usually came up with the answers I sought. I did everything the hard way, because I didn't see the value of investing money I had earned from my time on something, which had an unknown outcome.

This was when online courses were starting to become very big in the online world. People were waking up to the fact that anyone could be a teacher if they had the knowledge and were willing to put in the effort to package it and sell it to others.

But I was super skeptical. Having come from the instructional design world at the oil company, I didn't know if these online courses were worth the money they were being sold for. I had just spent three years of my career working on multi-million-dollar training programs. Programs where entire departments were involved in creating the content for, entire subject matter teams were employed to develop the learning, and large learning agencies were hired to create the final course products.

I was skeptical of someone being able to bootstrap together their own course, and it having any sort of real world value or measurable, proven results at the end. Not everyone is an instructional designer, and I knew I didn't want to waste my hard-earned money on a course which wasn't created by an educational expert, who had real world experience in what they were teaching.

So, I didn't invest.

I continued to figure things out for myself, often the hard way, and spent two very busy years making no forward momentum in my business. No real growth in revenue, the same feast and famine cycles, the same hardships between doing the work and getting more clients.

It wasn't awful by any means - I was still doing work I enjoyed with clients I liked. But the feeling of stagnation was hard to shake. The feeling of not doing anything meaningful got stronger and harder to ignore.

But Then it Changed

In late 2012, I had been following a business advisor online and enjoying her blog articles and content. So much so I bought a few smaller priced items - specific business templates and guides. I saw good results from using these.

One day, an email from her landed in my inbox talking about how she was creating an online community coaching program, paired with an online course. At the word 'online course' I usually tuned out, because at this point I had convinced myself the quality of online courses were subpar at best, and I could learn more on my own.

I can't say why, but this one caught my eye and the value proposition was solid. She had a proven track record of helping business owners get over their own insecurities and start taking action, plus her coaching clients were always singing her praises.

I knew if any course was worth it - this one probably was.

I still didn't take action though. At the time, I was a bit stagnant in my business, and I couldn't justify the amount of money. That money was better spent elsewhere in my mind, and there was no way you could have convinced me otherwise.

And then, I won a spot in her program.

One day an email came into my inbox with the results of a contest she had held for her course launch. I can't even remember what I had done to enter the contest, but there was my name, in bright bold letters in her email, announcing the winner.

I had won!

I was over the moon with excitement, doing happy dances and waking my neighbors at ungodly hours with my screams of joy. It wasn't until that moment I let myself believe I actually wanted to be in this course. I actually *did* want to invest in myself and make changes to the way I showed up and how I ran my business.

But the money factor, the scariness of putting my hard-earned dollars toward something which wasn't even remotely guaranteed, had held me back.

As we progressed through the program, I was incredibly impressed by the way it was run and the materials covered. Here was a woman who had no background in instructional design, creating a course which actually got real results for the people who were taking action and implementing the knowledge into their lives.

Were there people who didn't see results? Sure.

There were a handful of people in the program who I never saw again, and they complained the whole time about not being able to figure out how this would work for them.

But there were many more of us who applied what we learned and saw measurable changes in our businesses because of it.

I experienced a big shift in the way I looked at investing in myself after this program. I saw how concentrated effort and attention, with an expert who knew the ropes, was much more valuable than figuring things out for myself.

And even though I didn't actually put money into the program, I applied myself like I did to make sure I wasn't wasting such an amazing opportunity. And it worked! I started getting more clients, I started charging higher rates, and I started feeling much less stressed about my business and life in general.

After one course, I was immediately a convert of online learning (and I haven't looked back since).

So. Many. Options.

Seeing the difference this one program had on my business, convinced me online learning was worth the investment - if you followed through with it, and applied what you learned.

This realization both turned around my own opinion on the power of investing money in learning and growth, but it also helped guide me in bringing my own instructional design services to the market.

One small giveaway changed my mind, and often it'll be something similarly small to help you learn this lesson too.

Since 2012 when this happened, the online space has changed

drastically, with everyone and their dog having an online course they'd love to sell you. I get the skepticism which comes from wanting to invest in yourself, of being hesitant about the cost, and making the right choice, when faced with so many options.

There are powerhouse courses we see everywhere once a year, and there are smaller courses open year-round. Every expert out there has realized courses are a very effective way to make money, and the barriers to entry are almost non-existent. This has led to a glut of online courses, and it can be hard to figure out which ones are worth investing in.

At last count, there are over 100,000 courses on Udemy right now, a popular online course platform. And that's just one platform. Being able to tell which ones are quality, and which ones are not worth our time, is the hardest part of wanting to learn and invest in ourselves.

We're busy and we have client work to do, so if we invest in ourselves and commit to taking the time to learn, we absolutely need to know the time and money we put into it will bring us a good return on investment.

That's why the online course world can be so frustrating to many service providers. We know the skills and knowledge we want to learn; we know how we would apply it to both our client work and our own business, but making sure we make the right decision on which path to invest in is a frustrating decision.

Once we start looking for other options besides courses, we get into the world of group programs, masterminds, mentorships, and one on one coaching. Each more confusing than the last.

Choosing one of these is even harder, because the investment is often much higher than an online course, and the commitment is more intensive in terms of time and attention. Some masterminds and group programs even require you to travel to meet with them in person. If you live in a remote area like I do, the travel and time needed to attend these events and in-person trainings can be hard to come by or might even be non-existent.

To say there are a lot of options for investing in ourselves, and that choosing between them is hard, is like saying the sky is blue. We all know this. So how can we make sure we're making the right investments in our business and in ourselves? Investments which will bring us a positive return, and won't leave us frustrated for wasting our time or money?

Deciding if Right Now is the Time to Invest in Yourself

The first step in investing in yourself is deciding whether or not this is the right timing for you. But wait, here's a spoiler. It's never the right time.

There will never be a perfectly timed release of an investment opportunity which will 100% work with your current situation. If there was, my perfect investment would be a 24 day retreat to a beautiful island, where I got to work hand in hand with amazing mentors and experts who worked on my business for me, while there was an included nanny and a private villa for me and my family.

Odds finding that are pretty slim, so we make due, right?

But knowing there will never be the perfect time is different than waiting for things to be perfect before you invest.

When we know things won't be perfect, we try our best to align the other parts of our life to support us. We shift things around so our project work and client responsibilities will give us the breathing room we need to get the most from our investment.

We'll make it work.

For the right personal investment, I've seen service providers move mountains to make it work, and I know you can too.

But it's not always the right investment at the right time, and there's a key distinction. The right investment at the wrong time can be made to work. We can move responsibilities, projects, and push things back to allow space for the right investment at the less-than-ideal time.

But how do we know if it's the right time for our investment? How do you know we can indeed move things around to suit our decision?

The first key to figuring this out is, of course, to look at our project or client load. Are we completely booked out? Or do we have some wiggle room? Can we save the wiggle room for ourself? If we're not completely booked out, and we can save that wiggle room for ourselves without our rent being unpaid, then that's the first hint the investment is feasible for us.

The second key is to figure out the rest of our schedule outside of work. Is summer vacation coming up and the kids will be out of school, leaving us with no childcare for two months? Is it close to the holidays and we had planned on taking some down time to recharge? If our schedule outside of work isn't too booked, the odds of our personal responsibilities conflicting with our investment are low, and a good indicator that this may be the right time to invest in a new program.

But if it's a season in our life where we have lots of extracurricular activities, or responsibilities outside of work, perhaps it's not the best time to dive into an investment we'll need to focus on in order to get a proper return.

Making Sure You're Committing to the Right Investment

One of the biggest fears I have before I invest in myself is that I'm making the wrong decision.

This is a pretty universal fear. We wonder if we're making the right choices when we choose peanut butter at the store, it's no wonder many of us are crippled with fear when it comes to laying down large sums of money for new knowledge with no inherent guarantee of a return on our investment.

At least with peanut butter, we can get a few tasty sandwiches out of the deal.

How can we make sure the decisions we make to invest in our growth as service providers is the correct choice for us? How can we guide our decision-making process, so we take in all the variables while still allowing a healthy amount of caution and making room for our intuition at the same time?

It's not as hard as it turns out, but it does take a bit of practice to hone the investment decision-making muscle. Once properly honed, this decision-making muscle will help guide us through the tricky waters of marketing tactics, false scarcity and hype to make sure what we're investing in is indeed the perfect fit for us, right now.

The Four Investment Guidelines

There are four major guidelines I use to guide my choices when it comes to investing in myself and my skills as a service provider.

I arrived at these after joining many programs, courses, and groups, which turned out to be the wrong choice. These guidelines have certainly been through the test of trial and error for a real service provider, looking to go from hired gun to Secret Weapon status.

Using these four guidelines, you'll be able to make the best choice for you when faced with the next big program launch or promotion going around. You'll be able to make sure not only are you making a sound investment, but you'll be happy with the returns after the fact, and not left with a bitter taste in your mouth, or a grudge against the waste of time, energy, or money.

Guideline #1: Does This Align With Your Values?

We all have career and business goals, but these goals are one or two steps below our values, and our values in our career and personal life will help us much more in the long run than our goals.

Our values are underlying currents in what and how we do things, and so can much better guide our decisions on whether or not an investment helps meet them. When we work against our values, we'll be fighting an uphill battle the entire way, not only learning something new, but fighting against our inner self who's yelling at us that they don't agree.

An investment which goes against our values will not only be a poor investment, but one we'll very much regret taking after the fact.

For example, one of my main values is creating meaningful relationships with people in my life. I do not thrive on superficial, or shallow interactions, and that's one facet of social media which completely turns me off. So when I was pitched a program about how to create automated messenger bots and the best practices to do so, I immediately knew it went against what I wanted my business vision to be.

I couldn't build meaningful relationships with people when I was automating the entire process. It made me feel physically ill to think of how people would want to connect with me and be greeted instead by an automated response that had no personality or couldn't understand the nuances of their messaging and requests.

The choice was clear in my mind, this was not the right investment for my business.

Before you act on investing in your business and in yourself, I heartily recommend doing some values exercises to discover yours. When I first did this exercise, it was very eye opening to me to discover what I truly valued. My actions, decisions, and the emotions around those decisions made a heck of a lot more sense when viewed through a filter made of my core values.

Guideline #2: Does This Align With Your Career or Business Goals?

Nestled comfortably underneath our values are our goals. These goals guide us in the daily actions we take, the projects we take on, and the clients we work with. Our goals define how we use our time, both in client work and outside of client work, and help to steer the ship of our business and career paths.

When we're thinking of investing in a new course, program, or training, it's important to make sure the investment aligns with our career and business goals. If it doesn't, that's a clear sign it's not the best investment for us right now. We might be getting looped in by marketing tactics, instead of following our own good sense.

Side note - I am a sucker for marketing tactics.

Even with my own career being largely comprised of creating marketing strategies and assets for my clients, I still get sucked in by a well-executed launch.

When I first started seriously investing in myself, I was convinced to purchase many products and programs, which didn't align with the goals I wanted to achieve in my business. But the high-pressure sales tactics and count down timers got me every time and I caved, purchasing something I didn't use, and certainly didn't need.

If I had taken a step back, and instead asked myself whether this program or training aligned with my business and career goals, I would have been able to resist the temptation when the answer was a very clear no.

But this question can also be a bit tricky, because there are technically two types of goals - our business goals and our career goals.

Are we purchasing this training or course to become better at a skill or strategy for our own business, or is this is something we feel we'll be applying to our client work?

Investing in training for our client work and career goals is much more straightforward and can be easily rolled into the expense category for training. There's very little need for justification on this one, because we can see how it will affect our overall career goals of acquiring new skills and becoming a more valuable Secret Weapon to our clients.

But investing, for the sake of our business goals, can be a bit trickier. There's more nuance and grey areas, because it hinges on our efforts to apply the investment in our business, and actually use it.

If I had a dollar for every course myself and others had purchased and didn't implement, I'd have a nice little pile of bills indeed. Business goals depend on the execution of the information, much more than career goals. If I become better at using a certain piece of software, that can save me time, and make me more efficient with my client projects. But if I learn a new marketing strategy for my business, and don't implement it, then it absolutely was the wrong investment.

In the case of the course I spoke about in the first guideline, about creating automated messenger bots, I knew it wasn't right for my business. It clashed with my own values of building relationships, and so I didn't invest in it for my business.

But yet, I still bought it. Why?

Because it was aligned with a career goal.

Being able to offer my own clients bot creating, and building services aligned with my career goal of becoming a one-stop marketing automation gal. I wanted to offer these services to my clients and learning from an experienced bot builder who had been doing it for some time made absolute sense. I bought the program and started building bots for my clients. This training has more than paid for itself since I purchased it, because I've used it to build bots for paying clients. So far, the training has had a positive ROI of more than ten times the initial cost - definitely a smart investment!

Take a look at your goals, and see which ones are career oriented, and which are business oriented. Will this investment help you reach one or more of them? If so, you have a good indicator that it's the right investment. If not, you have a clear red flag that perhaps this isn't for you right now, and you can walk away feeling happy you made the right choice.

Guideline #3: How Long Will it Take to See a Return?

How often have you seen ads with sweeping proclamations that you'll be able to earn six figures in six months? When's the last time you were intrigued by a program, promising you a certain amazing result from applying what they're teaching?

It's pretty common place nowadays, that every program, course, or training has an enticing hook used to get our attention. More often than not, it's based on a too good to be true result that we're inevitably drawn toward.

But what are the chance everyone who takes the program actually gets the same end result promised? Pretty slim.

The fantastic results we see many programs and courses touting are the outliers. Not everyone who takes a program is going to see the same results, or even any results, depending on the amount of effort they put in, and the level of follow through they have. How then, can we peel back the hype to make sure that even if we don't achieve the spectacular results the course promises, we do indeed see some sort of positive return?

The first thing we have to ask ourselves is if this will be helping us achieve career changes or business changes. If the course or training will provide career changes, such as a new skill set or a new type of service we can offer, then we can expect to see a return far sooner.

The beautiful part of skills and services is, once we know, we know. At that point, we can start applying this to our client projects right away. There's very little lag time between when we start offering the new skill and service, and when our clients start paying us to provide it.

Courses and programs aligned with career changes often bring a far faster ROI than ones aligned with business changes. We can use this to gauge the amount of time we can start seeing a return on our investment. In the case of the bot building program I purchased, I was able to pitch a new Facebook Messenger bot to a client by the time I was halfway done the course, and the new project more than paid for the price of the program itself.

When we're looking at programs and courses promising business changes, these are trickier to pin down in terms of the amount and speed of return on investment. Business changes, such as operational or systems, marketing and promotional strategy, leadership and business management - are softer skills which can have a huge impact in the long run, but are harder to predict when they'll become worth the initial investment.

That's not to say we should never invest in them. But rather, we should be aware that it will most likely be a longer time period to measure the specific returns we'll make.

For example, many of us service providers have taken a course or program dealing with one form or another of client attraction and closing. Whether it's social media, direct outreach, sales training, or branding - we can all agree they are indeed, very important to the running of a service-based business. But at what point can we say, "That's when my branding started working." Or, "This is when my social media strategy really clicked and brought in a new client."

These are very hard to predict and directly measure.

When you're thinking about investing in the next program or course, take a moment and identify which area you'll see the changes - either career or business - and make a logical assumption of when you can start to see a direct return on your investment.

If it's a career-based course, and you're pretty certain you'll see a return in a few weeks, you can account and be prepared for that. If it's a business change, and you think the changes will most likely take a few months to a year to see the results, you can plan for that, and decide if the initial investment is worth the eventual return.

There are no right or wrong answers to this part of the guidelines. It's more about what's comfortable for you, and whether this return on investment aligns well with your goals from the second guideline, and what you're comfortable with in terms of the length of return on your investment.

Guideline #4: Do You Have the Energy?

Energy is a funny thing. When I first heard the word energy in relation to business or career, I immediately thought of physical energy. How much of a physical energy level I had on any given day. But the real truth is, energy comes in a variety of flavors and we'd be remiss to focus entirely on physical energy, when asking ourselves the fourth and final guideline to deciding if an investment is right for us.

The first form of energy we need to consider is the obvious one - our physical energy levels. Are we doing what we need to do right now to keep our physical energy high? Do we have the time right now to focus on good food, good sleep, and physical self-care?

If we don't currently have the time to focus on this, then adding an additional obligation in the form of a new training or program is not the best decision. We need to take care of our money maker - ourselves! Because if we go down with the latest flu to sweep the nation, no one's there to give us sick pay, and we need to ensure our body supports the efforts of both our current project load, and our new investment.

If you feel as though you take care of yourself pretty well, and you're not too concerned about this new investment taking time away from your efforts to maintain and bolster your physical energy, then you're good to go.

The second form of energy we need to consider is mental energy. Are we currently under a lot of stress from our projects? Have we taken on more demanding or mentally taxing tasks, which may need to be taken into consideration?

In my own work, I know there are certain types of projects which are more mentally taxing than others. When I plan out an entire sales funnel for a client, I know I'll be using more brain power than if I'm designing a sales brochure. If we have more mentally taxing projects in our upcoming future, adding the additional strain of learning something new and implementing it might not be the best choice for us right now.

Whereas, if you're pretty confident the projects coming up in your timeline are business as usual and don't require too much more effort on your part, then it might be a good time to give yourself something to stimulate your mental energy.

The third type of energy we need to consider is money.

Yes, money is energy. It ebbs and flows, coming in and going out - just like our physical and mental energy. Our money energy is a key part of this decision, because not only do we have to be aware of how much return on investment (in the form of money), this new course or training may bring, we also need to consider how much of our own money we're spending to achieve the end result.

Do you have the funds in your bank account right now for this purchase? Are you reasonably certain that if you spend this money, it will be replenished in enough time to maintain your financial obligations?

Some people will give advice that you absolutely should never invest without having the money in hand. Others will say not all debt is bad, and if you're certain the investment will pay off, then feel free to go into debt to do so.

Personally, I'm somewhere in the middle.

I started off my business by going very heavily into debt, and while it taught me an amazing set of lessons I won't soon forget, it's not something I feel is completely necessary. There's no trial by fire merit badge you earn by climbing out of crippling business debt.

I don't regret many of the poor financial decisions from my past, but I do regret making them all in such a short time period. The cumulation of several years of not asking myself the above guideline questions before I invested in myself and my business, led to many poor investment decisions over the years. These poor choices left me at one point with over $60,000 in debt, and some tough decisions to make.

But even with this experience in my past, I can confidently say that not all debt is bad. I certainly can't say otherwise without being a pretty big hypocrite.

I have a mortgage and a car payment, I run my business expenses through a line of credit I try to pay off each month (but don't always succeed) and I frequently invest in trainings and courses purely on credit when I'm confident I'll see a return on them.

This is why making sure we have the right amount of money energy to say yes to an investment is a big part of these guidelines. It's easy enough to say yes, and then worry about how we'll pay it off at a later date. But when we take this into consideration as part of the other three guidelines in this chapter, we see, "do I have the money?" is the very last question we ask ourselves. Money is the final deciding factor, but by the time we get to the money question, we should have some pretty clear indications as to whether or not this is the right investment.

These guidelines have helped me make the investment decisions in myself and my business much easier and can be applied to any investment when you really think of it. You can apply these same questions to purchasing software or an online tool. You can use these to guide your investment into contractors or employees, and you can certainly use them to guide your personal investment decisions as well.

Four simple guidelines, which can help you ensure you're making the right decisions about investing in yourself. Using these, you can be sure your investments align with your values and goals, take into consideration the length of return on investment, and also the levels of various energies you have to commit to any large investment.

By using these guidelines, I've been able to both invest in myself when the opportunity is right, and steer clear of the shiny object syndrome I'm incredibly prone to.

A Secret Weapon knows they need to invest in themselves in order to grow - it's really a non-issue. But the key to being a Secret Weapon is knowing which investments to make and when, without getting caught up in the tactics and excitement of a launch promotion.

TL:DR

- Making investments in ourselves as service providers can be intimidating.
- There are a lot of online courses, trainings, programs, in person masterminds, retreats, and conferences we can invest our money into. Making the choice on which ones are worth it is the key to staying focused in our work, while maintaining growth over stagnation.
- In order to make sure you're making the right decision to invest in yourself, you need to take a look at your entire situation - starting with the amount of time you have and then seriously considering each one of four guidelines:
    - Does it align with your values?
    - Does it align with your career or business goals?
    - How long will it take to see a return?
    - Do you have the energy? (Physical, mental, and money energy)
- Going through these four questions will help guide your decisions as to whether an investment is right for you as a Secret Weapon, right now.

CONCLUSION

The journey from hired gun to Secret Weapon is constant and in flux. It's hard at times, rewarding at others, and sometimes can make you want to pull your own hair out in frustration. But overall, I don't think I would have changed my own journey down this path.

Looking back, I can see how everything which came before has led me to where I am today, and if anything had changed along the way, I don't know if I would be in this same spot, the same person writing this book to share with you what I know.

Being a service provider is a funny thing really. We work with real, live, honest to goodness people, and what we do is a direct fruit of our own labor, our own genius, and our own skill. But we often lose sight of just how talented we are.

By nature, service providers are attentive to the world around them, and this can often be our downfall in the form of shiny objects or concepts which attract our attention but turn out to be detrimental to how we work or our sense of self-worth. Our need to better ourselves, both in our careers and as people, defines us. It's our shining glory. But it can also be our downfall.

It's a double ended bear trap - some ideas can latch onto us and propel us forward in our career. Others can snare us and keep us stuck in one place for far too long. Knowing which one is which is the hardest part as we endlessly pursue the idea of being better - both for our clients and for ourselves.

It's this need to better ourselves that we can harness for our own good in forging ourselves into Secret Weapons. The path is not straightforward, but it is rewarding, and I find it follows set steps we can identify and use as signposts to guide us along the journey.

The First Step is Owning the Fact You Are a Secret Weapon

No one can give you this title. You need to claim it for yourself first and foremost. When we decide to walk this path, when we bring our actions into alignment, and we put to rest the internal conflicts of if we're worthy of this, we've hit the first signpost.

When we realize that this moniker, this identity, is one worth owning for ourselves, something small and subtle shifts inside of us. For some it's profound, for others it's a simple nod we're heading in the right direction - but for everyone it's the first step.

The Second Step is Complete And Utter Self Doubt

Sounds fun doesn't it? There's usually a period of about a week, maybe more, after you accept and acknowledge you're a Secret Weapon, and are walking around lighter than air. You're happy and confident and full of yourself.

Then the second signpost hits and you fall into a deep spiral of imposter syndrome. Who am I to claim this title? There's nothing special about me. How do I possibly differ from everyone and their dog who also offer this service?

The true mark of the second signpost is complete and utter lack of faith in yourself and trust me - it gets better. The key to getting through this stage is to feel the fear and do it anyway. Trite words uttered by someone on the other side I know, but they are nonetheless the truth, and most truths are simple and rage-inducing.

The majority of service providers stay in a vacillating dance step between step one and step two. They feel awesome, then they feel like crap, they feel like they're invincible, and then they feel like failures. Over and over again they bounce back and forth until they either quit, accept their place as a hired gun, or something happens to push them to step three.

The Third Step is Taking Your First Tentative Steps to Owning Your Status as a Secret Weapon.

This is usually facilitated by enough social proof you can't ignore it. Someone who is truly great at what they do, someone who runs their business well and goes above and beyond for their clients (which is you now right?), will inevitably get to this place where your clients give you the nudge to own your Secret Weapon status.

I will never forget the first time one of my clients first dubbed me with this title (thanks Megan!). It was ego-inflating, life-changing, and liberating, and it made me feel all warm and fuzzy inside. I didn't think it was a precursor to something bigger, but I knew it was significant. And it helped me finally accept I was great at what I did, and there seemed to be something different about how I did it that made my clients love me.

With evidence like this from our clients, how can we possibly ignore it? How can we possibly think we're imposters, when so many people outside of us are telling us we're great at what we do?

The third step is about accepting the reality of what is already going on around you and acknowledging your integral part of it all. Once you reach the last and final step, the imposter syndrome becomes easier to ignore, and the proof of your accomplishments become harder to refute. You are a Secret Weapon.

Sadly, There Are No Ribbons But There are Definitely Rewards

I'd love to say once you arrive there are ceremonies, golden awards, and a marching band to herald you into this new age of being. But sadly, I'm still waiting on mine, so I don't think it's forthcoming. The rewards are there, they might be subtle and hard to place our finger on at first, but they are there.

It's less a final destination with a big red X marked on a map, and more of a hard climb that suddenly gets a lot easier. You're still on the mountain, but the trail has gotten much easier. The rewards of shifting our focus from hired gun to Secret Weapon are numerous, and they fall into a few main categories.

Firstly, we tend to make more money. As a Secret Weapon you can charge higher prices and be happy knowing you will deliver the value those prices warrant.

Secondly, we work with higher quality clients. We can listen to everyone else complain about nightmare clients, and know deep down we are in fact, never going to have to complain about that again. In my opinion, this is worth more than the price of admission.

We also get to do work which fulfills us. When we get to this stage, we get to pick and choose our projects more carefully. There is far less of a need to take anything that comes our way. We can turn down the projects we don't want to do, aren't our forte, or we simply have a bad gut feeling about. That is freedom of a different sort, and it's absolutely delightful.

And lastly, we get a greater sense of working towards something, rather than feeling like we're on an endless slog day in and day out. The string of projects doesn't feel as though it never ends, but rather we can see how each project leads to the next, and how each client brings us one level up the ladder. Each week and month that goes by, we can see our skills increasing, our career expanding, and our business growing. It's far more fulfilling having a life based on growth rather than on motion.

I never would have thought this path could be so rewarding in so many different ways. I was simply looking for a way to not have to pay for daycare, and to actually be present while my little one grew up.

What I found was something so much more than that.

Nine years of walking down this path has revealed to me the complexity and nuances of creating a career and a lifestyle based on the quality of service and dedication to an idea that transcends what I do and who I do it for.

Being a Secret Weapon is not about the services you provide or the projects you create. It's about a way of being. A way of serving that entails far more care and attention than the average person is willing to give. That's why Secret Weapons are so rare.

But now you know the lessons I learned so harshly over those early years. I'm hoping you can avoid learning by experience, and instead learn by example. None of these lessons are hard per se. Their consequences are hard, that's for certain. But the implementation and execution of them is not.

When I was in the thick of learning them, it was difficult to see the very obvious answer to my problems through the pain, frustration, and the late nights. Certain people say hindsight is 20/20, and they're right… jerks.

But it's true, and if someone had handed me a book like this when I was first starting and said, "read this, it'll help," I think it would have saved me a lot of those frustrated tears and late nights spent trying to scramble to provide.

As you finish these last few pages and realize this journey to becoming a Secret Weapon is so very worth it, I want you to also know you are worth it. You have what it takes to be a Secret Weapon. You are worthy of completely changing the way you do business and are going to be able to forge the path of your career to accomplish great things in the coming years and decades.

I can't wait to see it.

RESOURCE LIST

For Business and Project Management

Dubsado
A project management, client invoicing, scheduling and great all in one tool for business workflows and client follow-ups (if you sign up using the link below or use code "secret weapon" you can get 20% off your first month.)
https://dubsado.com

17Hats
Contains invoicing, expenses, project management, contracts and a bunch more tools for a service-based business. Great tool but can be a bit of a pain to set up initially.
https://www.17hats.com

Bullet Journal Method
A simple notebook-based philosophy for to-dos and note taking. Popularized by Ryder Carrol and customizable to suit your needs.
https://bulletjournal.com

Omnifocus
An advanced to-do app with integrations with calendar and other platforms. I found it too complex for my needs but know others who swear by it.
https://omnifocus.com

For Automation or Processes

ProcessStreet
For creating and managing business processes - a bit of an overkill for a one person show but interesting, nonetheless.
https://www.process.st

Lucidchart
Less complicated that ProcessStreet and more focused on visual representation of processes and business flows.
https://www.lucidchart.com

Evernote
A digital note taking app that allows you to clip from web, save and tag resources and other features. Can be as s simple or as complex as you like.
https://evernote.com

Airtable
An online database platform for creating all sorts of searchable records.
https://airtable.com

For Contracts

Adobe Acrobat DC
Has a built-in signature engine you can use to send the pdfs you already use and get them signed.
https://acrobat.adobe.com/ca/en/acrobat.html

Hellosign
For simple contracts that you can send via email and have clients sign online. Can be tricky to set up advanced fields, but good for basic contracts.
https://www.hellosign.com

DocuSign
One of the original online document signature platforms. A bit clunky but does the trick and has some flexible pricing plans.
https://www.docusign.com

Financial Resources

Profit First
An excellent book by Mike Micalowicz on how to structure your business finances to focus on profit first, expenses second. I've used this successfully in my business for the last 2 years and have been blown away by its simplicity and effectiveness.
https://amzn.to/2oEr0vo

You Need a Budget
A great app for tracking finances (it has a different approach so be warned the learning curve is a bit steeper)
https://www.youneedabudget.com

Wave
A fantastic free invoicing tool that also connects with your bank accounts so you can track expenses.
https://www.waveapps.com

Freshbooks
Designed to be friendly to small businesses, Freshbooks is a great invoicing platform built with service providers in mind.
https://www.freshbooks.com

Tiller
Google sheet-based budgeting and expense management. They have a bunch of different templates and it's easy to create your own. Simple effective and connects with your bank accounts automatically.
https://www.tillerhq.com

Productizing Services

Brian Casel
The first place I heard this term and the best at explaining it in ways that can help you clearly put it into place in your own business. His course is amazing, you should definitely invest if you want to go deeper on this.
https://productizeandscale.com

ABOUT THE AUTHOR

Gabrielle Chipeur is a marketing automation specialist who's spent the last 16 years at the crossroads of design, technology and online education. Besides helping coaches put their business on autopilot, she's worked with Fortune 50 companies, international best-selling authors and world-renowned motivational speakers to grow their business and expand their reach.

Gabrielle started her freelance business 10 years ago when she decided to stay at home with her children instead of going back to corporate. After struggling with 6 years of stagnation that came from focusing on the wrong things while she juggled small children, client projects and a pesky need for sleep, she transformed her business and documented all the lessons she learned along the way in her book, *Secret Weapon*.

She lives just outside of the mountains in Canada with her family and a small menagerie of animals and when she's not up to her elbows in tech she's usually covered in paint or cooking up something in the kitchen.

www.ingramcontent.com/pod-product-compliance
Lightning Source LLC
Chambersburg PA
CBHW030617220526
45463CB00004B/1319